CAPTURED
BY THE
RISING SUN

Dan Miceli Lin

Phil. 3:10-11

Don Nixon

Phil. 3:10-11

CAPTURED
BY THE
RISING SUN

MISSIONARY EXPERIENCES UNDER JAPANESE OCCUPATION, 1941-1945

DARREN MICAH LEWIS

TATE PUBLISHING
AND ENTERPRISES, LLC

Published by Tate Publishing & Enterprises, LLC
127 E. Trade Center Terrace | Mustang, Oklahoma 73064 USA
1.888.361.9473 | www.tatepublishing.com

Tate Publishing is committed to excellence in the publishing industry. The company reflects the philosophy established by the founders, based on Psalm 68:11,
"The Lord gave the word and great was the company of those who published it."

Book design copyright © 2013 by Tate Publishing, LLC. All rights reserved.
Cover design by Allen Jomoc
Interior design by Jomar Ouano

Published in the United States of America

ISBN: 978-1-62854-106-9
1. History / General
2. History / Military / World War II
13.10.30

ACKNOWLEDGMENTS

In order to accurately relate the stories of missionaries interned during WWII, first-person articles, letters, books, and their missionary files have been meticulously reviewed. It is fortunate that so many left so much information concerning their time under Japanese occupation. Future generations must read their accounts so that their stories will never be forgotten.

Few have ever seen or studied these first-person accounts. Through the generous allowance of the World Missions Department of the Assemblies of God, hundreds of pages of first-person information were made available. Though Assemblies of God missionaries are the focus of this book, much information has been included from other denominations.

The Assemblies of God World Missions Department made more than four hundred pages from the files of these missionaries available. This information was invaluable to the research necessary for this project. Many of these files provided background information concerning culture, foods, terrain, and the relationships with Japan as they moved into war. Personal information about the missionaries and their families helped add a human aspect to the story.

Special thanks to Dr. Gary McElhany for his patient and wise counsel during the writing of this book. Thanks to my wife and family for their encouragement to fulfill my dream of earning a master's degree and to my mom who gave me a passion for history and who I lost during the writing of this manuscript.

CONTENTS

INTRODUCTION

No war is ever easy or pretty. General William T. Sherman once remarked, "War is hell." War is violent and often fueled by an intense hatred of individuals or ideals. Whatever the causes, wars have come; and advancements in weaponry and technology have created greater damage.

When World War I ended, many believed it to be the war to end all wars. Tanks, airplanes, and advances in machine gun technology, as well as the use of chemical weapons made WWI the most costly and territorially expansive war in history to that date. Many soldiers never recovered from their war wounds and prayed that war would never come again.

Remembering the hell of WWI, numerous Americans called for the United States to protect its own borders and leave the rest of the world to fight. Failed diplomatic endeavors in the Pacific brought the realization that if a new war broke out, it would indeed be a world war.

With the possibility of war in the Pacific, many in the United States were willing to simply hope for the best.

Opinions changed when US interests were attacked by the Japanese on December 7, 1941. Japan surprised the United States; and in so doing, they awoke the ingenuity and inventive spirit of a nation. President Franklin D. Roosevelt delivered his Day of Infamy Speech, and the United States Senate declared war on Japan.

To protect common interests, Germany, Japan, and Italy had aligned themselves before the United States entered the war. At the outset of the war, numerous nations throughout the world came together to form the Allied powers. Later, the United States, the British, and the Russians formed the primary powers. All three had interests in both theaters. The French were also played a key role in Europe, though their power was limited as France fell to the Nazis early on in the war.

Britain was the key to victory for the Germans. The island nation was repeatedly bombed to prepare the way for an eventual invasion. In the Pacific, Australia was a possession of the British Crown that she defended. The United States had many interests in the South Pacific including Hawaii, Samoa, the Philippines, and the Marshall Islands.

Russia posed a unique problem. By area the largest nation on earth, its rugged terrain, horrible weather, and expansive size were both a positive and a negative for its people. They possessed many natural resources and a large area for its population to move to should it became necessary; however, it was literally on both fronts. The Japanese could easily attack the Russian mainland, as was seen in the Russo-Japanese War, and Germany easily attacked the nation as it moved across Europe.

In order to overcome the obvious obstacles of a global war, the United States and her allies joined in a united effort on both fronts. This took a massive number of troops and a calculated counterattack that was slow at best. Across Europe and Asia, millions of civilians were held captive in their own homes and in prison camps. Their liberation became an important part of winning the war.

To their number were added American aid workers, soldiers, civilians on holiday, and missionaries. Those caught in the fighting had nowhere to turn and nowhere to go. Survival became the order of the day. For those in Europe, life was tough but most survived. Germany was a signer of the Geneva Convention; as such, conditions for prisoners of war and civilians far exceeded those in the Pacific. Japan was not a signer of the convention. The Pacific became a prison camp filled with disease, starvation, and the inhumane treatment of anyone who was not Japanese.

Stuck in this hell were many who had gone to Pacific nations in an effort to spread their faith. Missionaries, mostly from the United States, found themselves faced with little to eat, no contact with the outside world, disease, and death. From many denominations they came: Catholic, Baptist, Assemblies of God, Presbyterian, and many others—all with the same purpose, to share their faith.

One of the strongest presences was from the relatively young Assemblies of God. Formed in 1914, the Assemblies of God quickly became one of the foremost mission's organizations in the world. Their efficient structure and evangelical beliefs led to many being sent all over the world as missionaries. Leaving everything behind—friends, family, and fortune—they set out to win the world with a message of peace. Those stationed within the reach of the Japanese felt the brunt of Japanese brutality. Their common experiences forever link them together as they were captured by soldiers of the Rising Sun.

Books and articles tell the stories of those interned. Most make passing mention of religious workers in the area; however, very few recount the stories of missionaries. That is the sole purpose of this book, to preserve and tell their stories for future generations. Sharing stories such as these is the calling of the historian.

Great details of the military struggles that were occurring in and around those interned throughout the Pacific were written of. Many soldiers left stories of what the prison camps looked like, as well as how the interned were viewed by the US government, and the priority that was placed on their liberation. More than once, their liberation caused a shift in military strategy and planning.

Some information was also gleaned from Filipinos and Chinese in the areas of occupation. Their accounts add depth and an understanding of local culture, terrain, weather, and relationships. Many of these accounts came from those not interned; however, these watched and aided those who were, often to their own peril. Their brave stories of survival and aid should also be told. Because of their willingness to put their lives in harm's way, many missionaries survived starvation.

All of these stories come together to bring about a concise and accurate account of the internment of Assemblies of God missionaries in the Pacific. Their lives stand as a testament of the human will to survive. Their stories remind us of the hardship they lived through. Their experiences call all who read to remember what can happen when the world is catapulted into war. Their faith beckons us to share in their stories.

THE PHILIPPINES

At 7:53 a.m. December 7, 1941, bombs fell from the sky setting ablaze the American Pacific Fleet docked in battleship row, Pearl Harbor, HI. Four hours later as the fires still burned and the Americans calculated the cost, the Japanese launched another surprise attack.[1] This attack was aimed at the Philippine Islands. The bombs rained down on Clark Field sixty-five miles south of Manila, Baguio, and the islands of Corregidor[2], Davao, and Mindanao. Within ten hours, two hundred Japanese planes flew over Manila destroying the large fleet of American planes waiting on the tarmac for orders.[3]

Few Americans were shocked by the news of the attack on Pearl Harbor; meaning, it surprised no one that the Japanese attacked the United States; but it was expected to be an attack on American interests in the South Pacific. Even President Roosevelt expected an assault to be on the Philippines.[4] History has shown that he was not entirely wrong as the Philippines came under attack so quickly after the bombing of Pearl Harbor. Soon it became evident that the Japanese intended to cripple our fleet before it could aid our friends in the Pacific. In all, the Japanese had attacked the Philippines, Hong Kong, Malaya, Guam, and Wake Island all within a few hours of the attack on Pearl Harbor.[5]

The Philippines is a chain of over seven thousand islands situated south of Formosa (Taiwan) and west of Indonesia. The Filipino people have a rich heritage made up of native culture mixed with Spanish European and American influences. These islands were not new to conflict, but ill prepared. In the years following the Spanish-American War (1898), the United States temporarily took possession of the nation until the rule of law could be established.

The time of American influence within the Philippines was a time of great progress. Education expanded to reach the smallest villages on the most remote islands. Infrastructure was greatly expanded; trains, airports, roads, and clean water were a priority. Diseases were controlled by American vaccination programs. These wide improvements made by US officials and the fair treatment of most Filipinos drew the natives to support America.

All of these efforts did not necessarily mean that racial discrimination did not exist. President Taft's[6] reference to the Filipino people as "our little brown brothers" serves as a reminder of underlying differences.[7] This was a time of great discrimination for any that were not of European descent. The common attitude of the day is illustrated in a sign hanging near the entrance of the British consulate in Shanghai, which illustrates the typical views of race at this time. It simply read No Dogs or Orientals Allowed.[8] In spite of these underlying feelings, the Americans treated their Filipino friends with great respect.

Many of the US military commanders and political leaders were involved during the American occupation of the Philippines following the Spanish-American War. The-then-future-president William Howard Taft served as governor, and General Douglas MacArthur served as military commander of American forces. Dwight D. Eisenhower[9] served as a colonel on General MacArthur's staff for four years. His final year came to a close as Hitler began his blitzkrieg across Europe.[10]

During this time, General Douglas MacArthur was given the task of building a native army strong enough to maintain security. General MacArthur served as the military advisor to the Philippines. He was a hero of the First World War and a former chief of staff of the army. When the Philippines were attacked, General MacArthur was recalled to active duty, heading up the new US Army Forces, Far East. This new role placed him in command of the American troops in the Pacific and the Philippine Army.[11] MacArthur stated, "The Japanese attack came at least five years too soon."[12]

Though the attack came sooner than expected, the United States took immediate action. Eisenhower returned from the staff of MacArthur in Manila around Christmas of 1939. His knowledge of the defense plan of the Philippines gained him favor with General Marshall who put Eisenhower in the position of chief operations officer for the Pacific, a role he held until he was elevated by President Roosevelt and Winston Churchill to lead the fight in Europe.[13]

MacArthur, knowing that the Philippines would be attacked, developed a bold plan of action. Utilizing the ill-trained Filipino army and one division of the US Army, MacArthur met the Japanese attack head on. Marshall ordered the Philippines strengthened with tanks, artillery, planes, and the most modern equipment.[14] The support came too late.

As the war intensified in the Pacific, the Philippines proved to be a tough area for America to defend as many United States ships sat at the bottom of Pearl Harbor. Even with a collective force of 141,000 troops, the Americans and Filipinos could not hold the islands without naval and air support.[15]

The approaching Japanese Army cornered many American boys. The climate, jungle diseases, and the terrain proved deadly. During the time of American fighting in the Philippines, temperatures rarely dropped below seventy degrees and usually stayed in the high eighties to low nineties.[16]

The approaching enemy almost caught MacArthur and his staff as they fled the islands. At that time, the general uttered the famous words, "I shall return."[17] By 1942, the decision was made that the Pacific was too large an area for one ally to concentrate on. Churchill and Roosevelt decided that the British would defend India and Burma, while the United States would focus on the Philippines and Australia.[18]

Having met in Washington during Christmas of 1941, the Allied nations understood that the Philippines were the key to victory in the Pacific. They also decided that Germany was the key to ultimate victory. For this reason, Roosevelt agreed to the "Europe First Strategy."[19] Roosevelt believed that the defeat of Germany would lead to the fall of Italy and ultimately—Japan.

In the meantime, the Japanese could not afford to let the Americans remain so close to their shore. The many islands could be used as deployment bases for bombing raids over Japan, refueling stations for American ships, as well as training grounds for US troops; therefore, the US military must be removed or taken captive. The Philippines became the key to winning the war for both sides.

When the bombing began in the Philippines, the Japanese had fifty thousand troops waiting to land on the beaches of Luzon, ready to march to Manila.[20] As US forces evacuated, many military personnel and American civilians were left with no way off the islands and little hope of rescue. All they could do was wait and pray. Life quickly became very difficult for many. "On April 9, eighty thousand US and Filipino soldiers surrendered to the Japanese on Bataan and on 6 May 1942, the island fortress of Corregidor in Manila Bay was captured—ending all but guerilla resistance in the Philippines."[21]

The Bataan Death March serves as a reminder of the horrors of the war. American troops began the sixty-mile march from the Bataan Peninsula northwest of Manila Bay to internment camps in and around the city of Manila. Even the healthiest of soldiers were affected by hunger and disease. The results of injury also took a horrible toll. Thousands marched to their deaths.

In the city of Manila, the constant bombing brought great numbers of injured into the streets. War correspondent Annalee Whitmore was caught in Manila. A cable to *Liberty* magazine stated, "Schools closed. Bloody railroad bombings began. Drugstores had no more bandages, iodine. Hardware store empty except for clutching crowds around flashlight counters. Our grocery taped and padlocked."[22]

The loss of the Philippines as an American stronghold also signaled a military change in the European theater. "After the fall of the Philippines, the US Navy had to carry most of the burden."[23] The Pacific Naval Fleet had been injured greatly by the attack on Pearl Harbor. It required many months before this fleet was fully mobile again. During this time, foot soldiers were brought in large numbers to the Pacific. As the Pacific fleet was repaired, the navy once again took on the leading role in the war with Japan shifting a greater number of American foot soldiers back to the European theatre.

The Japanese takeover of the Philippines affected every aspect of life. Filipino citizens were basically under arrest in their own homes and work places. The national economy suffered as the Japanese took possession of whatever they could. Manufacturing, agriculture, the government, and natural resources were now at the disposal of the Imperial army. The American-recognized government of the Philippines evacuated to the United States. By the spring of 1944 President Manuel Quezon and his staff resided at the Grove Park Inn in Ashville, NC.[24]

Items of cultural importance were also seized by the Japanese. President Roosevelt created the Committee on Conservation of Cultural Resources in 1941. Many nations quickly followed suit moving their valuable artifacts and artworks into hiding. The Philippines were overrun so quickly that only five percent of their national library was saved.[25]

The Japanese interned many people across their realm of occupation; however, no place was as bad as the islands in the Pacific. Americans caught in China and even Japan itself suffered far less than the atrocities of those left behind in the Philippines. It is understandable that during a time of war, an opposing soldier captured became and remained a prisoner of war; however, many of the captured were not military personnel but civilians living among the Filipinos as doctors, lawyers, teachers, and missionaries. Missionaries who were sent abroad to spread the peace and love of their faith soon found their faith tested through trial, sickness, hunger, torture, and disease. So many religious workers, both Catholic and Protestant, were taken to the internment camp at Los Baños that one section of it was nicknamed "Little Vatican."[26]

It is their stories which have been forgotten. Innocent in their purpose yet guilty by their nationality, these men and women of faith sought to live life as best they could in the worst of circumstances with others interned. From many denominations they came. Some were called to the islands in which they were now enslaved; others serving in China had escaped capture by fleeing to the Philippines. Here they found themselves interned in a nation they knew little about and in worse conditions than their counterparts who stayed behind in China.

Their stories serve as a beacon of hope to all who find themselves in times of trial. Author Anthony Arthur calls attention to the experiences of these civilians in his book *Deliverance at Los Baños*. He states, "If 2,000 American civilians were rescued unharmed tomorrow by means of a daring raid from an enemy feared for its ferocity, it is not hard to imagine what an event for national celebration it would be."[27] Many of their stories were overlooked. Many more have been lost through the decades following the war's end.

The Reverend Leland Johnson and Helen Branch Johnson began their lives as missionaries within months of their marriage in 1933. Johnson first came to South China in 1929. Helen came immediately following their marriage.

Leland was born in Tecumseh, Michigan, in December of 1901. Helen was nine years younger, born in April of 1911 in Three Rivers, Michigan. The Johnsons spent four years laboring together in South China.[28]

After almost two years of raising funds in the United States with the General Council of the Assemblies of God, the Johnsons were asked by the Assemblies of God Foreign Missions Department to go to the Philippines in December of 1939 to establish an Assemblies of God national organization. Rev. Rosando Alcantara, a native Filipino pastor, recalls that the Johnsons had only been in the nation for two years when the war broke out in the Philippines.[29] During those years, Leland and the native pastors were successful in establishing the Philippines District Council of the Assemblies of God, with Leland serving as their first district superintendent. This organization served as the directing body for Assemblies of God activity in the Philippines.

Though the scent of war hung heavy in the air around Christmas 1939, as Japan already made advances in China, the Johnson's ship sailed through the port of Kobi, Japan with no incidence. The family arrived in Manila on December 24, 1939. There they celebrated a quiet, uneventful Christmas with new acquaintances and old friends. Over the next few months, the Johnsons found a home to rent and went to work establishing a strong Assemblies of God missionary presence in the region. This was not always an easy task. The

Philippines was and is strongly Catholic from the years of Spanish influence.

During the following two years, a Bible school, Bethel Bible Institute, was established in the city of Baguio by the Filipino District of the Assemblies of God. Here the Johnsons made their home. Early in 1941, other Assemblies of God missionaries came to help in the work, most redirected from China as the war had already begun there on the mainland. As the war moved closer to the shores of the Philippines, many missionaries chose to stay and continue their work. The Japanese attacked the Philippines on December 8, December 7 in the United States; escape from the island nation was no longer a possibility.

Leland spent much of his time traveling in those first two years. Interisland steamers were the easiest mode of travel. As he continued to travel around the nation establishing churches, Helen, Sister Rena Baldwin, and Sister Blanche Appleby[30] cared for the needs of the school. As the Christmas season of 1941 approached, the missionaries busily prepared for special services and activities at the school. Radio reports revealed the nearness of the coming war. It would prove to be closer than anticipated.

On December 8, 1941, I was out in my front yard trimming the Poinsettia bushes which lined the cobblestone steps. We had been taking very good care of these bushes, for they bloomed at Christmas time and were very festive decorations. Just as the trimming was completed, I noticed the increasing drone of planes. Looking up, I saw seventeen planes coming in from the north, passing just a little west of our house. I subconsciously counted them thinking, "Well, it is about time we received more planes." Just then, to my utter dismay, three of them peeled off and went into a power dive right over Camp John Hay....As I recollect now, I counted the entire group of seventeen planes, but not on one of them was the Japanese insignia. The sneak attack was well planned.[31]

Over the rest of that day, reports flowed in from all over the islands and from Pearl Harbor, HI. Great damage was done. The attack had been successful. The American and Filipino forces were caught off guard and ill prepared. Within days, the last of the American troops retreated from Baguio into the surrounding mountains. At the same time one remarked, "Japanese were swarming over the Lingayen Gulf area like so many millions of ants."[32] The advance of the Japanese forces came so fast, the people of Baguio chose to surrender in order to save lives.

On the day of surrender, many prepared substantial meals. For the missionaries, it would be their last American meal for three years.[33] Fearing the Japanese would loot their homes; they hid or buried valuable belongings. Air-raid trenches were dug in preparation of leaving their homes at a moment's notice, which they did, moving themselves to the

Brent School in Baguio. That night soldiers of the Imperial Army came to loot. According to Johnson, when asked if international law would be respected, the Japanese lieutenant stated, "All possessions were now considered as trophies of war by the Japanese."[34] Even the clothes on their backs now belonged to the Japanese Army.

Using the Brent School, internment began for most civilian Americans. The school was so crowded, the men had to take turns sleeping and standing. On December 29, orders came down that all of the internees should be prepared to march to an undisclosed location. With the children lined in front, the women in the middle, and the men at the rear, the march began to Camp John Hay.

The barracks at Camp John Hay were filthy from days of bombing. The water lines had been cut by the retreating Americans. With water at a minimum and flies by the thousands, the first wave of dysentery soon broke out. Food shortages began immediately. Oftentimes, the only way the missionaries stayed alive was by the Filipino people risking their lives to bring them food. Slipping fresh fruits and vegetables under fences or between cracks in the wall was very dangerous.

By February 1942, some conditions in the camp improved as prisoners repaired barracks; water became more prevalent, and a routine was established. The Japanese quickly disrupted this time of peace and small semblance of normalcy as each missionary was called before "the Gestapo."[35] Gestapo became a common term used by the interned for the Japanese interrogators. The Japanese military was intent on finding out certain information. The area also received more rain than normal. Many old timers from the area marveled at the unprecedented rainfall.

Many were called before the Gestapo. Each one returned quietly, being threatened not to reveal the questions. Rev. Rufas Gray, a Southern Baptist missionary, never came back. "As nearly as I can figure Rufas Gray must have been killed about twelve hours before I was called upon to sit in that particular heavy oak chair."[36]

Leland Johnson's questioning went on for eight hours with intense questioning for a time followed by a lull. As he walked into the room, one man served as interpreter, another as recorder, and another as a guard or "strong man."[37] After these hours of questioning, Leland was released. Most of his questioning focused on the role of a missionary, which was perceived by the Japanese to be another name for a spy.

A few days later, February 28, feeling the missionaries did not pose a threat to the empire, seventy men loaded into trucks bound for the Baguio Hotel. After a nights stay in relative peace, the missionaries were released to return to their homes. The Johnsons were the only ones to have a home to return to; therefore, the Japanese allowed all of the Assemblies of God missionaries to go to their homes.

In many ways, life at home was harder than life in the internment camp. Water was more readily available; however, soldiers watched every movement closely and food was scarce. The Japanese no longer provided even a meager meal of moldy, wormy rice. In order to survive, many borrowed money from the native people, gardens were planted, and permission was obtained to visit the public market once a week. This proved to be an all-day ordeal, usually resulting in a tense situation where many Japanese rifles were trained on Leland's head as he approached, unloaded his purchases, reloaded, and proceeded to the next check point a few hundred yards away, only to repeat it all again. On more than one occasion he was gone for so long, the other missionaries in the home became convinced he had been re-interned or killed.

October of 1942 brought about another time of great trial. Leland Johnson was arrested, detained with other missionaries, and taken to the Baguio cold storage building for another round of questioning. There the missionaries sat in a semicircle on the cold floor for hours a day. The guards threw a sticky ball of rice at them. Any man that dropped his ball was soundly beaten. Interrogators began their work on the third day. This time they were accused of aiding the Filipino guerrillas who had become more active over the past months in the mountains around Baguio.

The Japanese used many methods of torture including the water cure[38], hanging by the thumbs, and beatings with a large club. Five days after Leland was questioned, the jailer came to release them back to their families and internment at a new prison, Camp Holmes. During this time, rumors of

American victories in the Pacific spread. They did not know how or when American soldiers would reach the Philippines.

Camp Holmes was a relatively small camp consisting of five hundred prisoners. Holmes started well with six doctors, a dentist, and an excellent school.[39] Camp life was difficult; but at times, difficulty gave way to joy. One commandant arrived, limiting freedom. Soon another commandant arrived, granting freedoms. Food and medical supplies were in great need. Many suffered from tropical diseases to the point of death. Some relief came when garden crops came in or when Red Cross boxes were allowed to be delivered.

During this time, the Johnsons welcomed a daughter, Margaret Joy. She was one of many children born in internment. Even in the horrible living conditions of camp life, some happiness and normalcy was achieved. Births and holiday celebrations were among the greatest. Christmas was celebrated with much anticipation and joy. Handmade toys of all kinds were produced by the adults. At one time, a play was even performed to the great amusement of the Japanese.

By the end of 1944, American planes could be seen more frequently. The internees knew that liberation would soon come, unless the Japanese chose to execute the prisoners in advance. This was a common rumor and a frequent threat. On December 28, 1944 roll call was taken and the internees were told to prepare for a "sudden move of the whole camp."[40] At 3:00 a.m., orders came to load the trucks and march toward Manila. A day later, the internees arrived at Old Bilibid

Prison, a former prison used by the American and Filipino government following the Spanish-American War. The Prison was declared unfit for prisoners in 1939 and a new one replaced it.

"The prison compound was square, with 600-foot-long, 15-foot-high side walls topped with 2,300 volt wires."[41] Old Bilibid was a deplorable place. The prison was built to hold four thousand prisoners; at its height, twelve thousand internees called Bilibid their home.[42] The prison had been divided in half by the Japanese. One side housed military prisoners, many of which survived the Bataan Death March. The other side held civilian prisoners of war. Doctors, lawyers, and missionaries were held without regard.

"Under the Geneva Convention of 1929, the signatories agreed that should chaplains and medical personnel fall into the hands of the enemy, 'they shall not be treated as prisoners of war.' Japan was not a signatory."[43] Civilians at Old Bilibid were not allowed to converse with or see the military prisoners on the other side of the camp; however, evidence of their torture was everywhere, especially on the small hill just outside camp. Here thousands of graves were marked with small wooden crosses. Of the six thousand sailors and marines brought into the camp, only 257 were living when the Johnsons arrived at Old Bilibid.[44]

Conditions here were far worse than any other place the Johnsons had been. Food was almost nonexistent. Many believed that the Japanese intended to starve all the prisoners to death before they could be rescued. Body lice, fleas, and flies infested every corner of the camp. So many people were sick with dysentery that it was impossible to keep anything clean. Hundreds died in their beds covered in human waste too weak to move.[45]

At the beginning of the war, life at Bilibid had been far better than the Johnsons and others were experiencing. Still, life in the prison was tough. Guards used every opportunity to take advantage of the prisoner. One writes, "The guards let down baskets from their posts atop the walls; the vendors put in bananas, mangoes, molasses, and the like. The prisoners passed up money, most of which went into the pockets of the troops before it got to the sellers."[46]

While at Old Bilibid, the Johnson's little girl, Margaret Joy, became so ill they did not expect her to live for more than a few hours. Dysentery and dehydration wracked her little body. When the Johnsons arrived at the makeshift hospital, they were told that Margaret Joy had had 40 to 50 bowel movements in the last few hours.[47] Leland also became very ill with heart problems that same day.

Both Margaret Joy and Leland began to make miraculous recoveries by the end of that day. As people of faith, the missionaries believed these recoveries were symbolic of their coming rescue; and in two days, this belief was substantiated as the first wave of American B-17 bombers began their attack on the Japanese fortifications in and around Manila Bay. What joy this brought to the internment camp. "How delighted we were! We lived a thousand thrills a minute! We shouted; we danced the whole four hundred and sixty of us."[48]

Within hours, a loud commotion began on the streets of Manila. Prisoners sought any window or crack in the wall that might allow them to see what was happening. One gentleman had been able to hide his binoculars. As he reached the window, he realized the noise they were hearing came from American troops that had landed. "It's the boys, it's the boys, it's the boys I tell you, it's the boys," he shouted.[49]

At four the next afternoon, a series of explosions rocked those near the barracks. Hurriedly, the camp prepared for evacuation. "As members of F Company approached Bilibid, an enemy machine gun sprayed the boulevard and snipers let fly."[50] At four thirty, the American forces broke through and the evacuation began. By nine, the prisoners were safely behind American lines. Immediately upon arrival at the old shoe factory, American military kitchen staff began to prepare a meal for the weakest among them.

> The 754th Tank Battalion with gunner Tom Howard in Company A had checked in with the 37th Infantry Division and expected to face ferocious opposition as they entered the city streets. Instead it was more like a spontaneous Mardi Gras parade than a war.[51]

The next day, the prisoners were returned to Old Bilibid; it had been swept for land mines. Here they waited further instructions. A few days later as the prisoners were awaiting evacuation back to the United States, a great stir arose outside of the camp. Soon an American Jeep rolled into the compound carrying General MacArthur. He had come to meet the internees and pay homage to the thousands of dead Americans buried there.

March 10, 1945 became the day of ultimate victory for the internees. A short C-47 trip brought them to the boarding place of the *Admiral W. L. Capps* naval vessel. A few days later, the ship pulled under the Golden Gate Bridge. "Within a very short time we were in Mr. Berry's car and on our way to the Home of Peace. It was one of those perfect endings."[52]

The first American men to roll into the camp were from the Thirty-seventh Infantry Division also known as the Ohio Buckeye Division and the Forty-fourth Tank Battalion of the First Cavalry.[53] These divisions had literally stumbled across the internees at the Old Bilibid Prison. The American military had not known that any internees were held at that location. However they found them, the internees were rescued, and their personal war came to a close.

So many stories and experiences paralleled; however, there were differences in how detainment came. Johnson, as the leader of the Assemblies of God missionary group, endeavored to keep contact with those under his leadership. This was harder than it may seem. The Japanese came and went as they wished, releasing some and detaining others.

Missionaries were moved from camp to camp. Elizabeth Wilson is one whose story followed a different track.

Though their experiences cannot be separated, the accounts of these missionaries relay different details and opinions of life as an internee. Galley overall paints the Japanese in a more favorable light than Leland Johnson. This difference may come from the intense interrogations the men underwent. All internees approached the breaking point from malnutrition and starvation; however, many of the men underwent great mental strain as they were interrogated.

Elizabeth Wilson was born on September 26, 1911 in Lubbock, Texas. Wilson first received missionary appointment from the Assemblies of God to Northern China. The trials of missions work in China were hard at best. World War II had already begun in many areas of China before the Christmas of 1939. At this time, Wilson was celebrating the holiday in Peking with other missionary friends. To add a more American feel to the celebration, the ladies made stockings for the children and a traditional meal.

This season of hope that brought with it so many questions about the future was peaceful and blessed nonetheless. Caroling, gifts, and a beautiful dinner all came together to make that Christmas special for those six thousand miles from home. Little did they know how radically their lives would change as the scope of World War II grew.

As the Japanese's hold on mainland China grew tighter, many missionaries were moved to the Philippine Islands perceived to be safer, at least for the time being.[54] Here they settled into life as best they could. New missionaries, like Wilson, took classes at the College for Chinese Studies. As they prepared for school on the morning of December 8, 1941, Elizabeth heard loud footsteps echoing down the hall toward them, followed by a loud knock. Opening the door, missionary Robert Tangen said, "Girls, Japan has just bombed Pearl Harbor."[55]

There were nine Assemblies of God missionaries and their families serving in and around the city of Baguio, Philippines at that time, including Wilson and the Johnsons. Their lives changed in radical ways. General MacArthur once called the Philippines, "The key that unlocks the door to the Pacific."[56] They knew the war was eminent. Wilson recalls that, four hours after Pearl Harbor had been hit; the first wave of bombs fell on the Philippines.[57]

The apartments the girls and the Tangens rented seemed to them a place that would easily be bombed. It was decided the Tangens would move in with the Leland Johnson family and the girls would look for a small place nearby. Though they now lived on the outskirts of town, dangers still remained. Thousands of natives and American civilians filled the streets as they sought safety higher in the mountains near the missionary homes.

Baguio was the summer capital for the Filipino government. The mountains provided much needed relief from the summer heat and humidity of Manila.[58] It was also the home of the Philippine Military Academy. At the outset of the war, the academy closed as all the students were drafted. These two facilities added to the strategic and mental importance of the occupation of Baguio by the Japanese.

Strafing by low-flying planes was a constant problem. A civilian defense corps formed to aid in spotting these planes before they reached the city.[59] Danger was at every turn. All kept a bag packed should evacuation to Manila be warranted. Another was packed should word of evacuation ships come. In the end neither occurred. The American leadership decided that all the Allied civilians be moved to a single location for protection. Three locations were used in Baguio: the Baguio Hotel, the Baguio Country Club, and the Brent School.

Many of these civilians imprisoned themselves just before Christmas 1941. What a difference there was between that last Christmas in China and the next few in the Philippines. Air raids and other distractions became common during that first Christmas as internees. By December 27, the Japanese made it to Baguio. They were now prisoners of war.

"Because of the number of women and children, several men went down to meet the Japanese. Late in the afternoon, the news arrived that the brave 'Flag of Truce' committee had contacted the Japanese advance troops. Baguio surrendered without a shot being fired."[60] Soon the Japanese came to take possession of their cars. Having assured the internees that they would not be molested, the Japanese left stating that they would return in the morning.

A few hours later after drinking, the Japanese returned. In order to protect the children and single women, the group gathered in a small location. Many became sick due to the lack of air. During this time, the Imperial Army took everything that was worth taking from the scared internees. With machine guns trained on them little could be done. Possession of firearms by any, they were told, would result in death for all.[61] With baited breath, they waited the outcome of the search. Soon the command reassemble came. There they found many of their possessions thrown all over the floor. The remaining night was long and sleepless.

The prisoners spent one more weary and hungry night at the Brent School. The next afternoon, orders came to march. Japanese with rifles and bayonets at the ready led the internees to Camp John Hay. Many began the march with strength and arrived in weakness from lack of food. Wilson recounts, "At the outset of the march the little boy boasted that he could carry his truck with his little finger. Before he reached his destination, he cried out that he could not even carry himself."[62]

The march to the camp began with heartache. In an act of extreme cruelty and mental warfare, the Japanese separated the children, women, and men. Children as young as fifteen months old were forced to march and carry their own belongings. Mothers wept as the children began the march. Thirty minutes later, the women left. Eventually, the men caught up to the women who had caught up to the children.

All were taken to the same place, Camp John Hay.[63] Camp John Hay and Camp Holmes were both American military posts near the city of Baguio, used to house the American missionaries before the war's end.

American ingenuity was at work in daily life. During a short time of release between camps, one of the missionaries removed an electric motor from his washing machine and used it on a hand mill. This allowed him to grind rice and corn into flour for bread as well as peanuts for peanut butter, and native coffee beans.[64] Soap was made by hand and sold to make extra money to purchase food and needed supplies.

Early in November 1942, the Assembly of God missionaries were rearrested and sent to join others at Camp Holmes. The buildings here were already crowded. The population of Camp Holmes jumped from 396 to 513 overnight.[65] This taxed the already strained food supply. "Camp Holmes had a very high class of personnel. There were two hundred missionaries, counting families."[66] These two hundred lived here for two years learning what it really meant to be interned as conditions continued to worsen. Wilson had one letter reach her family during this time.

Dearest Mother and family,

It's wonderful to be writing you again. I am in good health and am still not very thin. All our missionaries are well and we thank God for His care over us; in fact, we have increased numerically, having two new members, Margaret Joy Johnson and Robert Ernest Tangen, both born since the war started. They are healthy, strong, lovely babies. At present we are at Camp Holmes, which overlooks a beautiful valley and a series of mountains dotted with lovely pine trees. For beauty, it is an ideal spot. We have plenty of rice, native vegetables, bananas, etc., to eat. As far as we are financially able, we can purchase extra fruit, eggs, etc. from Camp Stores. Most of our missionary group were released temporarily to assist in conducting our church services. Our church work seems to be making good progress. For the last year, however, most of us have been back in concentration camp. There are over 500 people here at Camp Holmes. We have a school, a hospital and we conduct regular work detail. I am a vegetable worker. In my leisure time I am studying New Testament Greek.

Please remember me to the church, and to other friends. Also Gladys Knowles and Doris Carlson would appreciate your writing their mothers. I hope you are well. You know you are constantly in my prayers and thought. Give my love to all my friends. We'll be so glad for a word from you.

As ever
Your loving daughter
Elizabeth Galley[67]

The setting of Camp Holmes appeared beautiful and peaceful. Life inside the camp was anything but beautiful or peaceful. In April 1943, the internees at Camp Holmes learned that the internees at Santo Tomas in Manila had almost self-rule. This illustrated the difference from being in the guerilla territories in the mountains and the city that was safely in Japanese hands. This new revelation caused those at Camp Holmes to push for greater freedoms. Their petition of the Japanese commandant resulted in a camp leadership committee being formed; this committee aided in the betterment of camp life as well as serving as negotiators with the Japanese.

Everyone in the camp had a job. Tending vegetables, mending clothes, and barbering are examples. Their work remained hard but truly meant survival. "The Japanese did not like the American women. They thought they were badly spoiled. One day, the camp interpreter, a woman who formerly had been a missionary to Japan, was talking to the Japanese commandant. He saw an American couple going to wash their clothes. Thinking the woman was receiving assistance; he asked angrily if the husband was helping his wife with the laundry. His feelings were relieved when he was told that the wife was helping her husband with his laundry."[68]

For Galley, the holiday season of 1942 brought back memories of the Christmas spent in Peking with friends and in freedom. Christmas in the camp was harsh, but they made best of the situation. Weeks of planning allowed there to be a better meal than normal as small food stocks were collected from those receiving mail or those obtaining from outsiders. All the adults joined the celebration by creating gifts for the children of the camp. Galley, still having the stocking from Christmas 1939 in China, happily shared it with Robert Tangen born in internment.[69]

Along with the celebration of Christmas, other aspects of life had some normalcy. Religious life was relaxed after a new commandant arrived. Services by the Assemblies of God missionaries, as well as Seventh Day Adventists, Lutherans, and Roman Catholics were held. Other areas of life also became more relaxed. Internees were allowed to raise goats for milk and pigs for meat. Following the Christmas of 1942, the Red Cross delivered boxes. What a welcome sight. Personal care products as well as food items were enclosed. These items were a welcome supplement to their usual provisions, but it did little to change the circumstances of those in the camp.

The next few years moved on in much the same manner. The camp operated in an orderly fashion, each one fulfilling their job. Sickness was still present, and food was still lacking. As internment grew nearer to an end, news of American advances came more frequently. Hidden radios reported from the West Coast of America, causing hope to rise in the hearts of many internees.

Christmas 1944 came and went with the same weariness of every other day in the camp. The only highlight for them was the delivery of mail from home, for many the only letters they received during their entire internment. Still for those striving to make it another day, letters from loved ones offered a glimmer of hope and made a special gift for Christmas.

A few days following Christmas, many of the Americans at Camp Holmes noticed large numbers of Japanese loading on and off trucks. By December 27, 1944, it became evident American troops were on the advance. Around the New Year orders came to move the camp from the mountain area of Baguio to Manila. This long trip was very tough for so many who were deathly ill. Their intended destination was the Old Bilibid Prison built by the Spanish during their rule. Galley described the prison as a wagon wheel; the main buildings in the middle with barracks like spokes all the way around.

Old Bilibid had a reputation for its horrible conditions. Japanese cruelty was immediate. Injured Filipinos were ordered to march to Bilibid Prison following the fall of the Philippines. On the way, their bandages unwound causing injuries and hemorrhaging. Many died within yards of the prison gate.[70] "Bilibid was used by the Japanese as a transit camp throughout the whole period of their occupation of Luzon."[71] Transit camps gave the Japanese time to find more permanent locations for prisoners of war.

Though tough for all prisoners at Bilibid, it was especially hard for the soldiers. Military prisoners were forced to march everyday to the port area of Manila to work on the docks. Others were forced to work at local airfields and as house servants for Japanese officers. This forced labor combined with a lack of food added to their physical decline. In the beginning, food at Bilibid was fair, quantity and quality had not yet suffered. Small coconuts, bananas, sugar, and eggs could be purchased. As the war went on, food and money to purchase food became more scarce.

Bilibid developed as a prison for lifers, murderers, and rapists. "Given its reputation, the use of Bilibid prison was also intended by the Japanese as an act calculated to humiliate and denigrate the Americans in the eyes of the Filipinos."[72] They also forced the troops originally taken to the prison to march three miles out of the way in order to bring further humiliation.

At Old Bilibid, internees faced the worst conditions yet. Sickness and disease were even more prevalent. Dysentery and dengue fever kept the camp hospital overflowing. "The only bright spot in their sordid existence was the systematic daily American bombing of the places of military importance around Manila."[73] These daily bombings brought so much hope to those suffering behind concrete walls.

As time progressed, American bombing raids became more prevalent and fiercer. One day, the sky was filled with American planes. Suddenly, antiaircraft fire hit one of the planes. In the midst of that happy sight, realities of war came home once again. "Rescue was coming, but at what price?"[74]

"At the end of January 1945, American forces in their drive for Manila had liberated Cabanatuan, and they reached the outskirts of the capital a week later."[75] The Japanese had no intention of giving up Manila. "A fierce battle for every house on every street began. Bilibid prison and Santo Tomas internment centers were on the very front lines."[76]

Galley recalls that on the evening of February 3, 1945, the Filipinos began to yell. The Americans were coming. "Mabuhay![77] Mabuhay! Victory! Victory!"[78] The sounds of tanks and explosions sent shock waves across Manila Bay. The rescue of all American civilians was a top priority. MacArthur sent word to the First Cavalry, the Thirty-seventh Division. MacArthur had intercepted orders from Tokyo. Thousands of lives had to be saved.

By sundown, American troops fought all around the camp. At that point, American soldiers still did not know where all the prisoners were located. Orders came to secure the Old Bilibid Prison. "Imagine the astonishment of the sergeant who was sent to reconnoiter the old Spanish prison when he saw several hundred American men, women, and children standing about in an enclosure."[79] With the prison secured in American hands, their long ordeal came to a close. Within weeks, most Americans were flown or sailed back to the states. The end had come.

Like Wilson, Blanche Appleby and Rena Baldwin's story began much as the others. Both worked under the leadership of Leland Johnson; however, as the war progressed, their story took a different turn. They found themselves in one of the harshest camps in the Philippines in the midst of one of the greatest military rescues of the war.

Rena was born in Morrow County, Ohio, in August of 1891. Blanche was born in August of 1887 in Pendergrass, GA. Both of "the Girls," as Leland Johnson called them, had served a missionary term in China prior to being sent to the Philippines. Affiliated with the Assemblies of God, Rena and Blanche were sent to Baguio, Philippines, to work at the Bible school established there.

Their story in the Philippines starts much the same as the other missionaries appointed there. Life in a new culture was an adjustment, but it was one they wanted to face. The establishment of the Bible school and the training of the native students were of utmost importance. It was a job they both took seriously and greatly enjoyed.

The Assemblies of God, Baptists, and the Catholic Church had a strong presence in Baguio. In the convent, the nuns gathered for morning prayers on Tuesday, December 23, 1941. The telephone rang. The head of the American community brought the dreaded news. "Sister," he said, "we've had a meeting here in the Pines Hotel, and I want to tell you what we're going to do. The Japanese are coming up the mountain and right now are in the outskirts of the city."[80] Seeking the protection of the Geneva Convention, the city surrendered.

When the Philippines fell on December 27, 1941, Rena and Blanche chose not to intern themselves with the others at the Brent school; rather, they chose to seek assistance from close Baptist missionary friends who lived nearby. Their hopes of being overlooked were dashed as Japanese soldiers searched the city for money, cars, and other valuables. Rena and Blanche soon found themselves moved to the school with everyone else. Here they spent several hungry and sleepless nights.

A few days later, word came that they were to prepare to march to a new location. The long march to Camp John Hay proved to be a struggle. Having had little sleep and less food for the past several days, physical weakness was already setting in. Arrival at the camp did little to boost their moral. The camp was dirty and wet. Small portions of food were provided, but clean water was not available for three days. Loss of weight and sickness from disease came quickly to the camp.

Five weeks after arriving at Camp John Hay, all of the missionaries were called together and told that they would be released. The Assemblies of God missionaries made their way to the home of Leland Johnson. During this time, food was in very short supply. With little resources to purchase food, most were forced to work as they could. Rena made extra money by teaching music lessons to the Filipino children in the area.[81] This did little to ease their need for food.

In June of 1942, Rena and Blanche made arrangements to return to their home. This decision altered the course of the war for them. They were soon separated from their friends. The following November, all of the missionaries were re-interned, except for Rena and Blanche. By some oversight of the Japanese, they missed them.

Many of the older internees were allowed to remain at their homes, though the Japanese closely monitored them. Armbands were given to these people so that they could freely move about the city. Rena and Blanche did not draw attention to themselves by seeking armbands. Not having bands to wear indicated prisoners in their own homes.

"Some time later came an order that all aliens must re-register…The Lord timed our going and we went into the city with a company that had armbands. Then when we arrived at the registration office, we asked for armbands and were given them the next day."[82] This allowed them to move more freely around the city.

For almost two years, Rena and Blanche lived quietly. Local Filipino pastors and neighbors would sneak food to them, often risking their lives to do so. In July of 1944, formal internment came once again.[83] Rena and Blanche were taken to the Los Baños Prison south of Manila. This was the site of one of the most daring rescue operations of WWII.

Los Baños was a resort town named for its baths. Located on a large lake, Laguna de Bay,[84] the Japanese established the prison camp on the grounds of an agricultural college in 1943, forty miles from Manila.[85] The agricultural college, made up of fifteen school buildings, five dormitories, thirty small cottages, and a sugar mill[86] sat one mile from the village. Palm trees and mango trees grew abundantly. The faculty homes were surrounded by extravagant tropical gardens. It was a beautiful setting. The reflection of Mount Makiling in the lake was breathtaking.

It seems almost odd that so much misery and death could come to an area teaming with life and beauty. Many of the men volunteered to be moved from Santo Tomas Prison Camp to Los Baños, knowing it was a better location. In the end, those at Santo Tomas fared far better.[87] Internees were brought from all over the area including eight hundred from Santo Tomas University. The numbers at Los Baños reached around 2,144 with three quarters of them being American. There were also British, Dutch, Canadian, Australian, Polish, Norwegian, and Italians.[88]

Life at Los Baños proved to be much worse than Santo Tomas. Food was scarce, disease was rampant, and the constant change of Japanese guards led to much apprehension. "Life at Los Baños took a nasty turn in 1944 when a set of particularly brutal Japanese guards took over. Deaths from disease, starvation, and even the occasional execution became the norm."[89]

One resident of the camp recalls that water came in very short supply. "Mount Makiling to the rear of the camp supplied only twenty thousand gallons daily at present, with a tiny reserve of ten thousand gallons. There was barely enough water for the 2,500 native residents of the area: already the water was rationed, the main valves being turned off at night."[90] The feeding of more than two thousand individuals who had little money also proved to be a major problem. As the war dragged on, this issue turned into a disaster for the camp.

Rena and Blanche called Los Baños home for the final eight months of the war. Rena recalls that their food quality and supply appeared to be in direct proportion to American advances in the area. When the Japanese were winning, food came in greater supply; as American planes appeared over the Philippines with frequency, "starvation rations"[91] were given. Wormy rice, tomato leaves, and sweet potato leaves made up their diet. As they could, the internees added edible weeds to help manage their hunger. A normal day's diet amounted to one thousand calories, barely enough to sustain life. "The dogs and cats that had previously roamed the camp disappeared, and small boys looked for lizards beneath the stilted cottages for lunch."[92]

Weakness and desperation became the constant companions of most in the camp. Rena and Blanche testify to the support of fellow missionaries and how that helped keep their hope alive. Rena says, "I can remember a day just before deliverance came when I was so weak I lay on my bed and thought I could not go any longer; but a Presbyterian missionary opened the Bible and read aloud from Psalms, and as she read the words of the scripture were just life to me, and I became wonderfully revived in spirit and soul and body."[93]

Mental strain was a major problem. "The great and immediate danger to be confronted at Los Baños, once survival itself had been assured, was idleness."[94] Work details helped deal with the psychological stresses of internment. After a time, the civilian directors of Santo Tomas and Los

Baños were sent back to Japan. "Now the same military men who were responsible for the Bataan Death March, for the camps at Cabanatuan and Palawan where seven out of ten Allied soldiers would die before the war was over, were in charge of the noncombatant civilians."[95]

Planes flew over Los Baños from the south, beginning the constant bombing of Japanese forces in and around Manila. The Americans were on the move. The sight of the bombers brought "hysterics of glee" to the internees and "obvious signs of panic" among the Japanese.[96] A few hours later, the camp executive committee was given charge of the camp. The Japanese soon left the camp, leaving explicit instructions that all internees were to remain in the camp. A two-month supply of food was left, but many began to forage for anything they could find in the village.[97]

In July of 1944, General MacArthur met with Admiral Nimitz and President Roosevelt at Pearl Harbor. Nimitz had formed a plan to attack Japan through Formosa neglecting the Philippines entirely. MacArthur argued against this course of action. In part, he cited the large number of American troops and civilians interned there and his promise of return. The decision was made that the battle for the Philippines had to be fought, no matter the cost. The president and Nimitz agreed.

As plans were formulated to free the Philippines, plans were also made to rescue the interned across and throughout the islands. General MacArthur chose the Eleventh Airborne Division to lead the rescue of Los Baños. This decision went directly against General Eisenhower's advice. Eisenhower had found that the use of paratroopers cost too many lives during the liberation of Sicily.[98]

During the time the internees were in charge of the camp, they learned of the Battle of the Bulge, the reelection of Roosevelt, and the coming end of the war in Europe. This news brought great hope for the future. Hope was reinforced in their minds on January 9, 1945. That day, the loudspeakers in the camp broadcasted a radio transmission from KGEX. "This morning January 9, 1945, General MacArthur led sixty-eight thousand men of the US Sixth Army in a landing at Lingayen Gulf, one hundred miles northwest of Manila. The battle for Luzon has begun!"[99]

Hope is fleeting in times of war. One good rumor or turn of events could boost the morale of the internees. In the same way, one action could pull that fragile hope out from under them. January 13, 1945, became just such a day. At three in the morning, the Japanese returned to Los Baños. Four days later, the Japanese guards executed an American prisoner.[100] Others had been shot before, trying to escape. One prisoner, George Lewis, was shot while attempting to return to camp. No one had been executed within the camp until that day. Terror gripped their minds.

A meeting between Filipino guerillas took place in the mountains on the same day the execution occurred. This meeting included three men who had escaped from Los Baños the night before. Their report helped the American ground forces, led by General Swing, understand the importance of rescue. Swing had received an urgent message on February 8 that they were to move on Los Baños as soon as possible; February 19 was chosen.[101] A two-part plan for liberation was adopted. One force would go directly to the camp. Another would strike the Japanese around the camp to prevent reinforcements.[102]

Due to problems with air support, the date moved to 7:00 a.m. on February 23, 1945. Other problems also needed to be worked out. "Los Baños lay more than fifty miles from the nearest point of the eleventh's planned route north, across steep mountain ranges infested with Japanese troops."[103] Ground troops from the 511th prepared to take out the guards before the first paratroopers hit the ground.

An amtrack gunner recalls, "At 2:00 a.m. 23 February, loaded with two companies of troopers plus artillerymen, jeeps and guns, we set out across Laguna de Bay toward Los Baños on the southeast shore. We were told paratroopers would jump at dawn."[104] Commander of the Eleventh Airborne, Major General Joseph Swing, called for the attack to occur at 7:00 a.m. while the Japanese prepared for the roll call of the camp.

The Eleventh Airborne flew over Los Baños. Others moved near the camp and along the beach two miles away. They were guided by local guerrillas.[105] Soon paratroopers landed all over the compound. It was 6:58 a.m., Major John Anderson's plane was the first to reach the drop zone. The drop was so successful that the Japanese troops were still doing morning exercises as American troops rushed past them to secure the weapons stock.

It was a chaotic scene as tracer bullets split the morning air. Grenades exploded with the sound of Imperial screams. Japanese soldiers sought any way of escape, with Filipino guerillas in pursuit. "To Sister Louise the sky seemed full of white parachutes, glistening like angels wings in the early-morning light. Almost immediately the nuns[106] heard shots, and the battle for the camp was on."[107] The 188th Glider Infantry joined in the liberation of Los Baños.[108]

The Los Baños rescue was daring. These men were dropped twenty-five miles behind enemy lines. "We heard firing and suddenly the word went forth, 'Look! There are American soldiers.'"[109] While the amtracks made their way to the camp a 75 mm battery kept the Baños garrison busy.[110] As all of this commotion was going on, a large platoon of American amtracks[111] arrived. The soldiers shouted, "Get out of here. Take all you can in your two hands, and then get into the amtracks!"[112]

As the amtracks arrived, many found that they were too ill to reach them. Catholic missionary, Sister Mary Trinita, had to be carried. She was almost starved to death and tortured on many occasions.[113] Rena Baldwin was the last one of the first group rescued to get on board an amtrack. With no room left, she knelt below the gunner.

By this time, the Japanese had converged on the only road leading out of the camp. The Americans had made plans in advance to cut across the open fields to a nearby lake. The convoy came under attack from sporadic Japanese fire. The hot shells from the machine gun fell onto Rena's back, burning her. Once safely in American hands, the amtracks returned to rescue others.

In all, 2,147 were rescued. The American commander had hoped to rescue 80 percent. In the end all were rescued. "One American soldier and a Filipino had died, while three internees were slightly wounded."[114] Of this General MacArthur stated, "Surely God helped us that day."[115] By March 8, the war was over for the last of the internees. They were safely on their way home to the United States.

Of the Los Baños rescue, author Eric Morris states, "But perhaps the most dramatic rescue of all was that of the civilians at Los Binos.[116] It was one of the most remarkably audacious and successful operations of World War II. They were rescued from deep behind Japanese lines, all 2,147 of them, men, women, and children."[117]

Rena and Blanche left first-person accounts of their ordeal. Rena left Japanese registration papers, letters from the American government concerning their rescue, clearance papers, letters following the war, postwar medical reports, and many other documents attesting to the trial she underwent, including hand-drawn maps of Los Baños and the surrounding area.

The rescue of those interned marked the beginning of their recovery. In a letter written by her American doctor, Rena was diagnosed with beri-beri disease[118] and tropical sprue.[119] Most suffered from the ongoing effects of internment for many years. In spite of all of the negative effects of internment, their focus remained on their freedom.

The internees found out later that orders from Tokyo directed the execution of the entire camp at 7:00 a.m. Many remember seeing more machine guns than usual lined up on the hill above the camp. If our American forces had been two minutes later, 2,147 internees would have been executed. Following the rescue of Los Baños, an estimated 1,400 Filipino civilians lost their lives as the Japanese retook the area, many of whom were tied to the stilts of their homes before the Japanese set fire to them.[120]

The liberation of the Philippines proved to be an important step in the winning of World War II for the allied forces. It was a costly win. America sustained 6,575 casualties during the battle of Manila.[121] Freedom came at a price, one that the interned had been paying all along. As the many prisons were emptied, celebrations erupted. The Army bandsmen played at Santo Tomas on February 24, just days after liberation.[122] Many of the internees at Old Bilibid Prison thought the American soldiers were Germans, due to their pot-style helmets adopted after they were interned.[123]

The landing of American forces on Luzon signaled the beginning of the end for Japan. Their forces became more desperate and more violent as they fought to hold on to any land they could. The landing on Luzon also "signaled the beginning of the first kamikaze[124] attacks of the war."[125] This desperate act took the lives of many young American boys in the last days of the war.

American forces saw the destruction and terrible effects of the Japanese all over the South Pacific. Their atrocities and violence toward all enemies was only rivaled by the German hatred of the Jews. Of the twenty thousand American troops captured in the Philippines, half died before 1945.[126] It should be understood, as with all wars, many of the common soldiers were only following orders at the peril of their own lives.

This also, on occasion, reached to the top. Even Hirohito had no immunity from the anti-peace faction after Japan's surrender. When General Douglas MacArthur asked the emperor point-blank why he hadn't taken a stand against the war earlier, Hirohito drew his forefinger across his neck in the universal symbolic gesture meaning "I would have been cutting my own throat."[127]

It took a massive force of American troops, joined with Filipino guerillas, to free the Philippines. General MacArthur used a force of two hundred thousand men, supported by a large naval fleet of five hundred vessels to conquer Leyte alone.[128] Freedom swept across the South Pacific. With defeat only a matter of time, Japanese soldiers turned to cruel tactics. Food supplies shrank and the ferocious treatment of prisoners increased.

Many of the ultimate plans of the Japanese came to light after the war such as those found by the Manila Navy Defense Force. Point four of a major directive from Tokyo stated Japanese soldiers should kill Filipinos within homes that were already scheduled to be burned, in order to aid in the cleanup of the bodies. Point five directed all men and women to be killed. The document stated, "All in all, our aim is extermination."[129]

With total extermination as the goal, thousands found themselves in the way of the Imperial army. Death, torture, and disease followed every area that the Japanese occupied. "Of the 26,000 American military men held prisoner by the Japanese during World War II, more than 10,000 would die; by contrast, all but 1,000 of the 46,000 American military held by the Germans would survive."[130] As the Japanese began their retreat from Manila, thousands were left dead. A conservative estimate was around "100,000 people killed."[131] This astounding number helps the modern reader understand the carnage.

It seems the Japanese dealt with their own men in a similar fashion. One writes, "They had little time for troops wounded in action…There were stories of bed ridden Japanese soldiers who were murdered by their doctors."[132] Failure and dishonor were not feelings the Japanese possessed. This ancient and proud culture never recovered militarily.

With the help of the United States and her allies, the Philippines drove on a road to recovery following the war.

Shortly after Manila was liberated, Santo Tomas University reopened. Many American and Filipino military personnel signed up for classes.[133] Servicemen learned basic Tagalog in order to greet Filipinos, pickup girls, or find "where Japs are?"[134]

The Eleventh Airborne played a decisive role in other battles in the liberation of the Philippines, including the Battle of Manila.[135] During the entire Battle of Luzon, they leaned heavily on local guerillas due to their limited numbers.[136] The Eleventh became some of the greatest heroes in the liberation of the Philippines.

On the home front, wives and mothers anxiously waited for their loved ones to return. One mother wrote,

> Dear Douglas—
>
> We too, have our maps in the "bulkhead" over the kitchen radiator. I have just put up the geographic map of your part of the world and have just put the pins in Leyte. Last night after the 11:00 news broadcast we heard General MacArthur direct from the Philippines, as the flag was raised and he put the islands back under legal rule. It was quite thrilling to hear.[137]

One soldier remembers the celebration on Manila as the American forces came through. Years of Japanese occupation and cruelty had come to an end. The Filipino people showed their gratefulness to American soldiers. "Out of nowhere

Filipino men, women, and children descended on the tired Yanks....They ran out of their houses and apartments handing out coconut candy, chewing gum, cigars…and anything else… they could give us. Pretty girls ran up and threw their arms around the sweaty…Yanks and kissed them."[138]

Much of normal life was slowly restored across the Philippines following the Allied victory there. For many American soldiers fighting and interned, mail service had been disrupted with the fall of the Philippines. General MacArthur set up his headquarters in Australia during this time. Mail sent to those interned went there. It was MacArthur's policy that all letters from home be answered by a member of his staff, giving as much detail to the families as they could.[139]

Morale at home and abroad sank during the war. Families had no way of knowing the fate or whereabouts of their sons, unless they received a fateful visit from the gentlemen in the green cars. Americans on the home front did what they could to support the troops abroad. One woman developed and implemented a plan to deliver dirt from all of the forty-eight states in small bags to the soldiers in the Philippines. Her letter to General MacArthur instructed that these bags be placed all over the Philippine Islands.[140]

At the beginning of the war, American attitudes toward the Japanese grew negatively stronger. From the internment of Japanese Americans in the United States to the prolific use of the derogatory term, "Jap," Japanese racism was prevalent.

As the war came to a close and the atrocities propagated by the Japanese became more widely known, this racism only increased. One soldier who had taken part in the liberation of Old Bilibid Prison wrote, "I looked upon them as being inhuman because of atrocities that I saw. I disliked the Japs and always will."[141]

Soldiers returned to the United States with vivid stories of the horrors of war and the ravages of jungle diseases. The close, often hand to hand, combat of the Pacific theater brought scars to the body and the mind; scars that would take decades to heal, if they ever truly fully did. Combat fatigue was common. Bill Alcine with the Seventy-Seventh Infantry Division says this of a medic he saw, "His hands were shaking badly. 'I feel okay,' he kept saying. 'I feel okay, but I can't stop trembling. What the hell is the matter with me?' He looked as though he were going to cry. The other medics tried to comfort him, but it didn't do any good."[142]

The fighting with the Japanese was a "take no prisoners conflict."[143] So many Americans found themselves trapped as MacArthur retreated from the islands. For many of these, the mental strain was insurmountable. MacArthur understood the necessity to rescue as many prisoners as he could as quickly as he could.

While it is true that most American civilians were interned across the Philippines, there are stories of escape from the islands. In his book *The Rescue*, author Steven Trent Smith recounts the miraculous escape of a group of forty

Americans. Most in this group belonged to the Presbyterian missionary association. For three years they hid in the mountains, avoiding the Japanese Army. Frequent moves allowed them to stay one step ahead of the enemy. Their heroic struggle and ten-day march to the sea culminated in their evacuation to Australia by a US submarine.

Survival in the jungles and mountainous areas of Cebu was fraught with danger, starvation, and disease. Their courage to survive and take care of themselves is a testament to the human spirit and to the strength of their character. In the end, their three-year ordeal became one of the greatest stories of evasion.

The struggle for the Philippines and the lives interned there developed into an epic battle. Though the US government continued to impetrate the Japanese for the release of American civilian prisoners, most were rescued by the military as the tide of war turned in favor of the Allies. However freedom came, for those interned, it could not come fast enough.

CHINA

The old and proud cultures of Japan and China have been at odds throughout history. Both races viewed the other as inferior; however, the sentiment ran hotter with the Japanese at the outset of World War II. Four years before the bombing of Pearl Harbor, Japan's aggression toward the Chinese came to a head.

China and Japan had a long and heated relationship. Both nations sought superiority in Asia, especially at the dawn of the twentieth century. Japan began to show aggression toward China by the mid-1930s, having already taken Manchuria. This act caused great concern to China and her people knowing that Japan had expansionist aims in the area. On July 7, 1937, fighting erupted between Chinese and Japanese soldiers near Beijing.

On the fourteenth of August, China bombed Japanese warships near Shanghai. By late August, Japan occupied most of northern China. Soon the southern port cities and the

Yangtze area were taken. Surprisingly, this action was done in opposition to the Japanese emperor's wishes.[144] For some reason, he resisted the idea of the Japanese occupation of the Chinese mainland.

The atrocities committed by the Japanese in the Philippines and other areas of Southeast Asia paled in comparison to their treatment of the Chinese. Their racially charged hatred of the Chinese fueled mass murder. More than three hundred thousand were killed between the years of 1937-1938.[145] The number killed throughout the occupation reached into the millions.

Horrific pictures of Japanese brutality survive today, depicting many ways civilians were exterminated. One such picture shows a family being buried alive. In others, Chinese are used for Japanese bayonet practice. Atrocities such as these only fueled the anger and hatred the Chinese already felt toward their oppressor.

During the earliest days of Japanese aggression, it became evident to many American religious organizations that their missionaries would need to be moved for their own safety. Most were redirected to other nations in the South Pacific. Still many chose to stay in China, believing God would protect them and they could be of help to the native people.

China is one of the largest nations on earth with one of the greatest populations. It has a rich heritage of technology and ancient religious beliefs. To the modern reader, it may seem foreign that a people with such a long and grand history could be viewed by its neighbors as nothing more than dogs. The emperors of China reach back thousands of years. Their culture is truly diverse with cuisine, language, and culture unique to its different areas.

Agriculture and the arts form the basis of their society. The Chinese are also known for great inventions: gunpowder and the byproduct fireworks stand out. Most are also familiar with the beautiful pottery they produced, the most famous of which developed during the Ming Dynasty which stretched from 1368 to 1633. The Chinese are also well known for their development of military tactics. Military historians are aware of China's long history of defense and innovation. Sun Tzu's *Art of War* is widely held as the foremost book on ancient military strategy.

From the Great Wall of China to the Forbidden City, Chinese architecture is unique and beautiful. Many innovations developed here, including buildings that could resist damage from typhoons and earthquakes. Shipbuilders also made great strides in producing large seaworthy ships. In recent years, some historians have developed the belief that the Chinese developed one of the earliest seaworthy ships. Some have even suggested that the Chinese became the first to visit the continent of North America.

The terrain and weather of China is as varied as its people. High mountains and deep valleys cover the Chinese mainland. Their climate makes it the perfect place to grow crops such as rice and tea. The wide and diverse production of fruits and vegetables should lend itself to having more than enough for the Chinese people; however, the over population of the nation as well as ill weather often caused great need. This was only made worse by an occupying army that appeared only too happy to take all they could from the already stressed food supply.

Cold winters and hot summers proved to be a challenge to those fighting and those interned here. Though diseases spread by bugs were not as rampant as in the island nations to the South Pacific, sickness from unsanitary POW camps and malnutrition took its toll on those interned. Psychological problems also arose from the horrible treatment of prisoners. Accounts of brutality and rape were rampant across British owned Hong Kong and mainland China.

As the Japanese edged closer to war with China, tensions ran high. The Japanese moved toward war with China by the late 1930s. Holding training and reconnaissance missions in and around mainland China only served to escalate the tide of war. In July of 1937, a-Japanese-force-performed exercises near the Marco Polo Bridge over the Hu River. As they crossed the bridge, they passed Chinese troops heading the other direction. A shot was fired, no one is sure by whom, and a minor battle ensued. The incident moved public opinion in Japan toward war.[146]

The Japanese occupation of Hong Kong was of great concern to the British. Hong Kong became a British possession following the Opium War of 1841. With Britain busy fending off the threats of Nazi Germany, the occupation of Hong Kong came fairly easily. The bombing of Hong Kong began December 8, 1941, following the bombing of Pearl Harbor, HI. That same day Japan also bombed Wake Island, Guam, Shanghai, and the Philippines.[147] The fall of Hong Kong allowed Japan to successfully hold British territory, a feat that Germany never accomplished, aside from the Channel Islands[148].

Prior to its fall, Hong Kong proved to be a point of great debate for the British. There existed a common belief that the Japanese military simply could not defeat the British. "Despite the fact that the British colony of Hong Kong was within sight of the Japanese in China, many British soldiers believed that the Imperial Army did not represent much of a threat…The British were superior to everyone and it was ridiculous for anyone to say that the Japanese were so good—some little nation like Japan couldn't possibly be better."[149]

Still, Japanese troops battle-hardened from conflicts in mainland China made early advances on Hong Kong. As the Japanese drew closer, the British withdrew to Hong Kong Island by December 13, 1941.[150] Churchill said, "There is not the slightest chance of holding Hong Kong or relieving it."[151] Churchill understood the difficulty of defending an island surrounded by the enemy. Its capture was only a matter of time. Unfortunately, because Hong Kong was a British possession, many British citizens found themselves caught with no way off the island and little hope of rescue for some time.

The surrender of Hong Kong came on Christmas Day 1941.[152] Atrocities by the Japanese in and around Hong Kong were immediate. One British officer recounts being lined up in front of a large storm drain. One man tried to escape and was shot in the back as he ran. The officer chose to fall into the drain. As he lay there playing dead, bodies fell all around him from above. They were bayoneted by Japanese soldiers. Soon a soldier came along with a rifle to make sure the job was finished. The British man pulled a dead body over his to hide.[153]

After such acts of violence, hatred of the Japanese only increased. Some soldiers and civilians reported killing Japanese as they could, simply to get back at them for the horrors they saw and experienced. Many British citizens residing in Hong Kong suffered greatly, especially women. Rape was a common occurrence. Women and girls were told not to resist. If they did not resist they would be let go. If they did resist, they would be shot.[154]

It should be noted that while mistreatment of westerners was a common practice, it appears not to be a mandate from the Japanese military command. "Appalling as the mistreatment of westerners in Hong Kong was in the first hours of the war; such cruelty did not represent Japanese policy, but random acts of brutality by individual soldiers and units."[155] For all the British residents of Hong Kong endured, it was nothing to what the Chinese lived through. Beating, robbery, rape, and the shooting of innocent civilians were the norm.

China led to many problems for the British and Americans. Officers had a lot of difficulty training the Chinese during the year of 1943. It seemed to one officer that all they were interested in was the procurement of weapons.[156] By that year, most of the major ports, cities, and farmland were controlled by Japan. The rest of the nation was split between the nationalists and the communists. The Allied forces sought to aid China enough to hold off Japanese advances until such time they could be defeated. The defense of the Burma Road was also paramount.[157] Despite all of their efforts, the Chinese Army was near collapse by 1944.[158]

For many westerners caught in the crossfire, telling the difference between their Chinese allies and the Japanese enemy was very difficult. One explained, "The Chinese will smile at you if you smile at them. The Japanese would not."[159] This may seem like a silly thing to be concerned about, but the propensity that the Japanese showed for rape and mistreatment made moving around occupied Hong Kong very dangerous, even deadly.

For American missionaries held in and around Hong Kong, life in prison camps became the norm for many years. Their lives held little value to the Japanese. Their welfare and health was of little concern. They, like others, were forced to eke out a living as best they could, all the while praying for hope to remain alive, protection to be constant, and liberation to come quickly.

In other areas of China, the effects of the Japanese invasion were different. As such, a study of the areas of China, consisting of Hong Kong, Northern China, and Southern China seems to be the most logical way to approach the subject. These are also the divisions given Assemblies of God missionaries assigned to the Chinese people.

The Assemblies of God had a strong presence throughout China before the war began. This is true for mainland China and Hong Kong. The British government acted very friendly to missionary activity of any kind in the area. As a "Christian nation," Britain sought any means it could to win the heathen to westernized culture. Many denominations had Bible schools, children's homes, and aid programs in the area.

By the winter of 1941, all Americans received orders to leave the Chinese mainland for the safety of Hong Kong. Japanese advances in the area made life difficult and dangerous. Lula Bell Hough was pastoring a church in Canton when the orders came. She left as told, bound for the village of Fanling on the Chinese mainland just across from Hong Kong Island. Isolated in this small village, Lula Bell did not hear of the advances of the Japanese army as Pearl Harbor, HI, and Hong Kong were both attacked within hours of each other.

It should be remembered that Hong Kong is made up of Hong Kong Island and an area on the mainland of China referred to as Macao. Macao fell fairly quickly as the Japanese continued their advance across the mainland; Hong Kong Island remained hard to conquer due to its isolation and its being surrounded by water. Eventually, the inevitable happened, Hong Kong fell.

A student at the Bethel Mission wrote of the bombing of Hong Kong saying,

> For three nights Hong Kong was ablaze. In the city lawlessness reigned. Mobs outside our building shouted, 'Let us go in and rob them.' The students and workers prayed day and night without ceasing. 'These Christians are poor people. They have no money. Let us go on to the others and not waste our time here,' some shouted. And our people were spared the ordeal of being looted.[160]

The Japanese occupation of Hong Kong brought missionary work to a standstill. No longer could the missionaries move freely about as they wished, crossing to and from the mainland. At the time of occupation, there were eight Assemblies of God missionaries and four children stationed there: Harland and Betsy Parks with their two daughters, John and Ethel Perdue, Abel and Nell Walker with their two children, Lula Bell Hough, and one other.[161]

Before the Japanese had fully occupied Macao and Hong Kong, missionaries often had interaction with the Japanese. Harland Parks reported moving in and out of the Japanese-held territories easily in the beginning. On one trip, he and a colleague had just crossed "no man's land" and entered a small village called Lo Pau. Here the city was in a grave state. The ravages of war could be seen everywhere. Nearly every home had been bombed out or burned by the resulting fires. Leaving there, they had to pass back into Japanese territory.

This practice of moving between occupied territories was common in those days of early fighting in China. Still the threat of Japanese anger was always real and evident. A few days following their work in Lo Pau, they returned safely to Hong Kong. "The political situation blew hot and cold as a result we in Hong Kong became complacent about the situation. We were suddenly jolted out of our complacency when the Japanese struck Hong Kong."[162]

John Perdue states that Monday, December 8 at around 7:00 a.m., Japanese planes began their attack of Hong Kong. Eighteen days of fighting finally led to the surrender by the British government on Christmas Day 1941. All westerners were now classified as "enemy nationals."[163]

Anarchy took over in the streets as young Chinese men turned to looting homes and businesses, anything to gain needed supplies and valuables. The missionaries had expected this result. With wisdom and foresight, they hid all of their valuables where they could not be found.[164] However, in the end, the Japanese took much of their meager possessions from them.

Families scrambled to find safety as the Japanese inched closer to Hong Kong Island. John Perdue placed his wife and children on a Chinese junk five miles off the coast of mainland China. "The sound of British and Japanese gun fire kept growing nearer. Bullets flew overhead like rain."[165] As the attack continued, John began to fear for his family's safety and knew that their food supply was running short. His only hope was to try to reach them. This, of course, was easier said than done as the Japanese now controlled all major roads and had instructions to shoot on sight anyone moving about.

Over the next few hours, John walked the ridge of hills above Hong Kong, once stopping to purchase food in a small village. In this village, the Japanese already had control. Unable to understand a Japanese sentry's orders, he was tied to a tree. Shortly, they escorted John to a nearby camp the Japanese set up. He reports seeing implements for the water cure about. After some time, an officer approached him with a written message that stated, "You are a spy of the British and Americans, and will be executed."[166]

As John waited to see what would happen, the Japanese changed guards to a man that spoke Mandarin. This gentleman showed a kind expression and a willingness to listen to his story. Having explained himself thoroughly, John waited for his fate. As he waited, the British began to shell the area. John was cut loose and told to leave the camp at once. He did, thanking God for protection in a tense situation.

The home of missionary Lula Bell Hough was ransacked by a drunken band of Japanese soldiers. One officer put his bayonet to the throat of a local church deaconess. His intention was to molest her. Lula Bell prayed, "Lord you can't let a thing like this happen. I know you won't."[167] Trying to help the young women, Lula Bell called to the other soldiers standing outside the house. This caused such a commotion and embarrassment to the officer that the young lady was let go as the officer slinked out a side door.

As internment came to the missionaries in the area, Miss Hough was the only Assemblies of God missionary in the Hong Kong area not interned at the Stanley Prison Camp.[168] She was interned at the Door of Hope Mission in Tai Po Market. For the first two weeks, those interned there lived on wormy, moldy, whole wheat. Hough lost thirty-eight pounds during her six-month internment.[169]

The completion of the Japanese takeover meant travel became even more restricted. In spite of this, John Perdue and his friend, referred to as Mr. Tom, decided to attempt visiting Taai O in order to check on the Christian community there. Many were found to be suffering from different illnesses resulting from their new diet. As the group began to have prayer in the little chapel, Japanese troops stormed demanding an explanation for why they met there.

Taken to headquarters, they were placed in a small room with no ventilation. The commander of this camp, Fung Tin, was known for being partial to beheadings. Mr. Tom, feeling the situation grave at best, wanted to hang himself with his own belt. John was able to talk him out of this. Within a short period of time, a voice came from outside the door; it was a familiar voice, one they recognized. This friend smuggled much-needed food to the two men.

All those found in the Taai O area were automatically considered to be spies. The commander ordered all spies to be taken out to sea and beheaded. Fortunate for those taken that day, Fung Tin was called to Canton and the boat used to take the prisoners to sea would not start. By late evening, the doors of the cell opened allowing John to leave. All of the others were beheaded two days later, including John's friend Mr. Tom. From here, John disguised himself as a refugee and snuck his way back to Hong Kong.[170]

The New Year found the Americans crowded in the Kowloon Hotel. Here the Parks and the Halls with their children all lived in one single room. Next door was a family with their grown daughter and a single man. The other room held six British men. At the outset of the occupation, the Japanese were not worried about convenience or who was where as long as all were accounted for.

Much like their counterparts in the Philippines, their food consisted of moldy musty rice with small amounts of cabbage, leaves, or radishes mixed in. Park recalls the entire hotel taking on the smell of musty rice. The Japanese would not allow anyone to open windows for ventilation.[171] They had even taken the time to cover the windows with newspaper so no one could look out into the streets. It is no surprise that those in the hotel found at least one room where the newspaper had a small hole in it. Someone would stand watch in the hotel as someone else looked through the hole. It was a desperate attempt to gain any information pertaining to their situation.

Internment at the Stanley Prison Camp came soon for all those in the hotel. The situation at the camp was hard at best. The diet was poor and getting worse, especially for the children who so desperately needed proper nutrition to continue growing mentally and physically as they should. "The little flock of Christians heard that we had been killed. However, as I peered from my window one morning, I heard someone calling my name."[172] The ladies below were able to report back to the local church that the missionaries had not been killed.

At the camp, a group of British school teachers began a school for the children. Each morning, all of the children went to school for half a day. Before leaving, the kitchen would prepare a small bowl of soft-cooked rice for them. "We managed one time to buy a pound of raisins and each morning thereafter our two girls were rationed six raisins each to help keep the rice down."[173] The diet in the camp consisted of three ounces of cheap rice twice a day. "Vitamin 'W' was the chief ingredient, the *W* standing for worms and wigglers."[174]

To add insult to injury, the camp warehouses were stocked to overflowing with food stockpiled by the government of Hong Kong. This food was to be used should they come under a blockade. Rather than sharing this food with the prisoners, which helped greatly in keeping them alive, the Japanese shipped the food to other areas for their own use. Starving Chinese in Hong Kong were also known to hijack the food shipments bound for the camp in an effort to save their own lives. This added even more stress to the food-shortage crisis.

Food was so scarce. Park recalls that their daughters came into their mother with a small can full of oily sand. Upon questioning the girls, it was ascertained that it was peanut oil the Japanese had spilled in a sandy ditch. The children filled many more cans with the sandy mixture which was then stained and boiled. A quart of clean peanut cooking oil helped improve the taste of the rice.[175]

Before their own internment, the Parks and the Perdues labored among the refugees of the war with Japan, which had begun in the late 1930s. Fearing the Japanese, many found themselves in Canton, an area that was already taxed and hurting. With help from the International Red Cross, two hundred were fed daily.[176] Now they found themselves in the same position as the refugees, needing food and needing help.

As the missionaries put it, miracles often happened in the Stanley Prison Camp. On one such event, shoes were greatly needed by John Perdue. It just so happened that within a few days, a local man known to him was selected to act as the interpreter for a Japanese official. This gentleman gave John sixty Hong Kong dollars. Shoes were soon purchased from a prison guard. There was also enough leftover to aid the other missionary families.[177] Occurrences such as this did much to keep their hope alive in those dark days.

Fortunately, for the missionaries interned at the Stanley Prison Camp, their time in China came to a close quickly. After just over six months, June 29, 1942, all were part of the reparation of prisoners with Japan. Within two months, they reached the shores of the United States aboard the *Gripsholm*[178]. Their ordeal came to a close fast in comparison to others caught in the throes of World War II. Lula Bell

Hough stated, "I was part of the first prisoner exchange by the United States and Japan, and it was an experience I will never forget."[179]

Lula Bell recalls the utter devastation of Hong Kong as they were preparing to be sent back to the United States. "When I left Hong Kong in June 1942, a thousand Chinese a day were dropping dead from starvation. Just about two months ago, news reached me that two-thirds of the Christians in Canton have died of starvation."[180]

The missionaries who returned to the United States did everything they could do to help the plight of local Christians throughout free China.[181] Money was collected and sent back, until Japanese advances severed ties with the hurting Chinese in early 1945. An update in an Assemblies of God pamphlet from 1944 read,

> We also are happy to advise that friends of Miss L. B. Hough of South China are assisting in getting funds through to many of our workers in the South China area, so that each month considerable sums of money are being forwarded to China. We feel that it is imperative that we maintain the flow of funds to China at this time of need.[182]

The trials of life in China only increased as the war with Japan dragged on. It is hard to say what would have become of these missionaries had they not been repatriated at that time. Many of the missionaries returned to China at the first opportunity they could. They took up the work that had been disrupted by the war and helped in rebuilding the community of faith which had been so badly affected.

Work with refugees and the starving across the Hong Kong and Canton areas became a priority. Shortly after the end of the war, communists took over all of mainland China. Hong Kong and Macao remained in British hands until 1997 when its possession reverted to the Chinese. Miss Lula Bell Hough returned to Canton in June of 1946 via Hong Kong Harbor. She quickly moved to her old home at Fan Ling, taking up the instruction and care of the children of the area.

The Halls also returned to China in 1947. They worked in and around Canton until forced to leave by the communists in 1949. Mr. Hall was assigned by the Assemblies of God to be the principal of the Ecclesia Bible Institute, Hong Kong in 1960.

The Perdue's returned to Canton in October of 1945. Traveling after the war proved to be dangerous for ships. As Mr. Perdue traveled to Hong Kong, his ship struck an underwater mine left from the war. Many lost their lives in this tragedy, Perdue survived though injured.[183]

The Parks also returned to their duties in Hong Kong. Mrs. Parks began teaching at the Bible College as Mr. Parks continued his ministry work. Mrs. Parks died in Hong Kong in March of 1961. At the time of her death, she led the local day school with more than four hundred students.[184]

The area of Northern China saw great missionary activity from the beginning of Chinese missionary work. By the turn of the twentieth century, missionaries established outposts all over the region. Larger cities saw the establishment of Bible schools, orphanages, and larger churches. This area developed into fertile ground for those working. Famine, natural disasters, and the communist takeover gave many opportunities to reach the hurting Chinese people.

The Assemblies of God had many missionary families in Northern China, more than any other region. From here missions work reached Manchuria, Mongolia, and many people groups. The spread of communism moved quickly across the region. The national Chinese government put many communists to death as they fought to overturn the free government of China. This takeover resulted in many trials for the missionaries appointed there. By nature, the coming communist movement was an atheistic regime. Its leaders had little use for religion of any kind.

As this civil war raged, the Japanese became an ever increasing threat to the fragile stability of the region. Missionaries now faced danger from the communist Chinese and the Japanese. Still their desire to help the local people remained great. Many missionaries made great sacrifices to help those in need. Marie Stephany was such a person.

Marie was born in Hungary in 1878. As a single missionary, she sought to aid the children of Northern China. During a famine in 1920, Marie opened her home to thirty children, sharing what little she had with them. This act of kindness established an orphanage in the Shanshi province which continued to operate after her retirement.

While Marie left a great legacy and lengthy information concerning her struggles with the communists and other crises that arose, very little is mentioned about her encounters with the Japanese. Her missionary file states that she returned to Shanshi in 1939 and was forced to evacuate three years later. "She was permitted to remain only three years before the Japanese invasion forced evacuation. Though she never forgot the treatment she received at the hands of her Japanese captors, Miss Stephany preferred to remember her happy days in Shanshi and the Chinese she won to Christ."[185]

Miss Alice Stewart's life and ministry is outlined in many letters and first person articles. Her experiences with the Japanese are more detailed than that of Miss Stephany's. It can be assumed that their experiences were similar as they worked closely together in the same area of northern China. According to Miss Stewart, the Japanese invaded the Shanshi province in 1937.[186] At that time, Christian women in the area took refuge in their mission, that is, all but one.

Miss Stewart writes of a woman named Mrs. Kuo who believed God would protect her. As Japanese soldiers entered her village, she remained in the open reading her Bible. Soon the soldiers, heavily armed, came to her home. As they stepped into the home, they noticed that she had not hid and sat reading something. She explained to them that she was reading the Bible. They left calling her a "woman of great courage."[187] The soldiers took nothing from her.

On December 8, 1941, within hours of Pearl Harbor being bombed, Alice Stewart and her coworker Henrietta

Tieleman were arrested by the Japanese. For three weeks, they were interned. With no explanation, they were released and allowed to return to their work. Miss Tieleman remembers that two months before their internment, the Japanese authorities advised them to leave for America.

The Japanese assured them that ignoring the opportunity to leave would result in their eventual deaths. As they packed their things, they realized that a concentration camp would likely be their destination, not the United States. The next day, the Japanese returned, asked a lot of questions, and left. This happened multiple times before they were finally taken into custody and interned for three months. "Consequently we packed and unpacked several times."[188]

Miss Tieleman was not taken with the rest of the missionaries, as she was traveling to an outstation.[189] Upon her arrival, police escorted her to another city that had soldier's barracks. For hours Tieleman was forced to wait with no word as to her fate or food. She was told to sleep in one of the officer's bed. Fearing that the officer would return, Miss Tieleman waited uneasily as drunken soldiers yelled outside the room. Finally, a soldier came to inform her about the war. She had not received news of Pearl Harbor yet. After a long wait, they escorted her to a room where she was allowed to sleep. Her nightmare had begun.

The ladies were interned for three months when, with no explanation, they were released. Trials of many kinds arose during this time. The Japanese occupation caused the shutdown of local banks, forcing them to make the dangerous trip to Peking. Danger from bandits, communists, and the Japanese waited at every turn as trains were stopped again and again for security checks, robbery, or simply as a scare tactic.

Their final trip came June 8 of 1942. It was Monday, and the daily routine began as normal. Japanese soldiers came to the house to question the ladies about nonessentials such as furniture and other household items. Still no mention was made of packing or moving. Three hours later, a truck arrived. They were told to be prepared to leave within three hours. Many from the local church came to help the ladies pack. From here, they were escorted to the port at Shanghai where they loaded them aboard the *Gripsholm* exchange ship bound for the United States.

Stephany, Stewart, and Tieleman fared far better than many missionaries in the region. Several Assemblies of God families were interned at length. Among them: the Hindle family, the Slager family, the Baltau family, the Hansen family, and the Kvamme family. Correspondence with these families became very rare during this time. Some letters, articles that they wrote before and after the war, as well as first person accounts of their internment give some detail of the nightmare they endured.

The Hindle family of Canada headed back to their work in Mongolia following their furlough of 1938–39. They had labored in this nation just to the North of China for more than thirty years. Traveling by way of Japan, they arrived in Peking to the news that they would not be allowed to continue on into Mongolia. With their plans changed, the Hindles joined the staff of the Truth Bible Institute in Peking. The war found them there.

On December 8, 1941, word reached the Hindle family that they now lived in Japanese occupied China. Mr. Hindle describes a scene of childish amazement as word reached the children. As they left the school heading to their homes, one shouted, "We shall meet in a concentration camp."[190] The school made preparations for a visit from the Japanese. Through some oversight on the part of the Japanese, the school had been overlooked. Several days passed before they arrived.

When the Japanese finally came, Mr. Hindle met with them and welcomed them to his school. After hours of questioning, the Japanese left, giving them permission to move about the city as they needed. This was a privilege they enjoyed for sixteen months until one person broke the rules by trying to escape the city. Due to this unwise action, the entire community was sent to the Weihsien[191] Concentration Camp in Shantung, China, March 17, 1943.[192]

Just prior to being taken to concentration camps, the Japanese called for all missionaries to assemble at the Peking Hotel. The purpose of this meeting was to force all property owned by them to be signed over to the Japanese. Missionaries from all denominations joined together in refusing to do so. The stalemate lasted for hours until one missionary suggested that they would sign as long as it was contingent on their mission board's approval. Not understanding the structure of these boards, the Japanese heartily agreed. Of course no board sitting in a free nation would agree to such a thing.[193]

The Civilian Assembly Centre, as the concentration camp was known, became the Hindle's home for six months. It was a Presbyterian mission compound touted to be the largest compound in the world. The area was beautiful, lying near a river and having many beautiful trees. In this time, they endured many hardships, but none to the level of their coworkers in the Philippines. Food shortages and sickness were a problem; however, the local Chinese were allowed to sell excess food over the walls of the prison.

The compound resembled a small city. The internees had the benefit of the church, dormitories, and hospital on the grounds. Hindle recalls that the hospital was short on supplies in the beginning; however, "conditions improved later and it was not long before the hospital was ready for any major operation."[194]

Those in the compound made the best out of their situation. Rooms were small but protected them from torrential rains which came in July. On the fourth, a small creek swelled so much that it caused part of the outside wall to collapse. The fact that it fell on American Independence Day was looked at as an "ill omen"[195] by the Japanese.

At the end of August, spirits within the camp rose as reports came that 250 of them would be repatriated. With mixed emotion, those whose names were on the list began the process of packing all they owned into trunks. The day of departure came on September 14, 1943. "Never before had I seen pleasure and sadness so strangely mingled in such a vast sea of faces."[196] The Assemblies of God Missionary delegation were among the ones leaving with mixed emotions. They came to China to bring a message of peace. They now left under the duress of war.

Repatriation was a long process. Having been sent to the port city of Shanghai, they boarded the Japanese SS *Teia Maru* on September 19. The *Teia Maru*, built to hold eight hundred, was loaded with one thousand passengers. Their numbers swelled as the ship made two more stops to pick up those being repatriated. On October 15, they reached the city of Goa, India. Here they met the Swedish ship *Gripsholm*, which took them the rest of the way to New York City and freedom. Aboard the *Gripsholm*, they were able to enjoy their first hot meal in weeks.

When the ship reached the dock in New York, crowds of family and friends met them. Hugs and stories were shared all around. Those who had been liberated found they had been reported as killed. Hindle states, "Many of our loved ones suffered more at home than we did in camp."[197] Three times the Hindle's daughter heard they had been killed by the Japanese. Joy emanated their return.

Mr. and Mrs. Hansen were also working in Peking at the time of Japanese occupation. Their story closely follows that of the Hindle's. The Hansens wrote letters from time to time allowing their family and the mission's board to know they were okay. Mr. Hansen wrote much about their time aboard the *Gripsholm*, mostly of a religious nature. He also sent a letter from Rio de Janeiro while traveling back to the United States. In it he states, "There are 25 Pentecostal missionaries, counting the four children. We are a happy family…"[198]

Another family of missionaries also followed the Hindles, they were the Baltaus. The Baltaus left little information concerning their ordeal. What is known is pieced together from the writings of others and the occasional mention of the camp and the *Gripsholm* in Mr. Baltau's writings. From all indications, they were among those repatriated.

While the Japanese dealt with the Hindles, Hansens, and Baltaus in what seems to be a lax way, the Slager family had a different experience. On December 17, 1941, Japanese Navy officers arrested Mr. Slager. For the next five months, Mrs. Slager knew nothing of the whereabouts of her husband. He was kept in a room with another man. At the end of the five months, Mrs. Slager joined her husband at the Tsingtao camp before being moved to Weihsien. They were interned together for three years. During that time, they lived in a twelve-by-nine-foot room.

Mrs. Slager wrote, "There are community kitchens, and dining rooms of a sort. Many of us have done extra cooking on stoves made of bricks and tin cans-when we had anything to cook."[199] Occasional Red Cross packages helped supplement their food supply and from time to time the Japanese increased their portions. "We have had liberty to move freely about in the camp daily until 10:00 p.m. We have appreciated this liberty."[200] The Slager's reported that they never suffered hunger in those days, but the Japanese became more unpleasant as the end of the war drew nearer.[201]

At the end of the war, an American plane flew over the camp. Paratroopers brought the news of Japanese surrender. The Slagers were among the first 580 internees released by the American Military.[202] Following their release, Mr. Slager's medical examination showed that he suffered from several illnesses while in the camp. A few plagued him for a time after obtaining freedom. No matter what the conditions of camp, all those interned suffered the effects.

So many missionary families suffered the effects of internment that those lucky enough to avoid this reality are easily overlooked. In Northern China, Miss Anna Ziese avoided being interned, because she was a native of Germany and retained a German passport. Still life for her, as with all living through the tragedy of war, was not easy. Miss Ziese counted that time as the most difficult of her life. She also counted her freedom as a blessing as she had the ability to move freely among the hurting Chinese.

In Manchuria, another missionary family dealt with the effects of the Japanese occupation. Mr. and Mrs. Kvamme were living in Manchuria when the war began. By divine providence, they were spared internment in a camp. As the Japanese rounded up enemy nationals, the Kvammes found themselves joined with a large contingency of Italians. This group was sent to the concentration camp at Shantung; however, no room existed for them there. Thus, they were allowed to live in Tienstin for the duration of the war.

Their freedom allowed them to remain connected to the local Chinese churches throughout Northern China. They were also able to send word to the mission's board and families in the United States concerning the welfare of their loved ones.

While information concerning the internment of missionaries in Northern China is a puzzle pieced together from many sources, the fact remains that many were interned at least for a short time. For those living through the fear of the unknown, internment was real and beyond description. Those released to continue their work still lived under the watchful eye of the enemy. Though reparation came, life under Japanese rule was anything but easy.

South China, referring to Southwest China, is a large region consisting of mountains and great rivers. Tucked near Indo-China, Burma, India, and Tibet, missionary activity reached here early in the days of Christian expansion from the west. Southern China was considered inhospitable and dangerous, not only because of the mountains, but also due to the large numbers of bandits who roamed the areas and hid in the high country.

The Japanese made advance in this region by 1938. Their intention appeared not just to occupy but to open trade routes to other Asian nations, most famously along the Burma

Road. Assemblies of God missionaries in this area evacuated before internment came. Still many had less than favorable experiences at the hands of the Japanese, as bombing raids in the area were prevalent.

Among the missionaries there were Mr. and Mrs. Leonard Bolton, Miss Beatrice and Miss Thelma Hildebrand (known as the twins), Mr. and Mrs. Howard Osgood, Miss Lula Baird, and Lawrence McKinney. Of these, the Osgoods and Hildebrand sisters leave the most detailed information.

The twins tell of frequent bombings in the days before leaving China. They often had to escape their village of Kunming in order to protect themselves from the raining fire. As word came that Japanese foot soldiers were advancing toward their village, the twins flew to Calcutta, India.[203]

Perhaps the Osgoods had the most harrowing experience. Mr. Osgood records their ordeal in an article titled, "Under His Wings Shalt Thou Trust." Here he tells of an air raid of the city of Kunming. He and his household attempted to escape their home as the bombs screamed through the sky. Mr. Osgood and his daughter Anita rode on a tandem bicycle, which they had often used to travel through the city. Everywhere they looked the bodies of the burned and wounded lay around them. The date was December 18, 1941. Within days, the Osgoods escaped the country.

In his diary Osgood wrote,

> The panic in the streets was indescribable. We went slowly, watching lest we be trodden down. Broken rickshaws, spilled baskets, loud bawling, till we were just outside the East Gate. "The enemy planes have come!" We lay flat, face down, on the dirty sidewalk and prayed as we heard machine guns and the exploding bombs. It was soon over. We rose to run again, crossed the bridge…and were soon in the midst of carnage! Had we been two minutes earlier, we might have been right there where hundreds of dead and wounded lay all about us. It was terrible.[204]

As the war came to a close, the tremendous damages caused by the Japanese became more apparent. Cities all across China were leveled, food supplies were ruined, and millions of Chinese lost their lives. John Perdue states, "My body carries the marks of this tragic affair."[205] The same can be said of China as a whole.

While different parts of the nation felt the effects of the war in different ways, there were no areas that did not see and feel the devastations of war. Some would argue that the most lasting effect of World War II in China was the coming overthrow of the national government in favor of the communist Mao. The horrible conditions left by war had many in the nation clamoring for a new stronger government.

By the late 1940s Mao and communism swept the nation. Some would also argue that the terrors of the communists rivaled that of the Japanese occupiers.

In the end, the Chinese people rebounded like many other nations. Cities were rebuilt, economies stabilized, locals planted fields, and babies were born. Life in China slowly returned to normal. However, because of the rise of communism, all of the missionaries eventually left. Many took up work in the surrounding nations which had also been ravaged by war.

JAPAN

The treatment of the interned in the South Pacific islands was the most brutal. In China, it was strangely calm by comparison; and perhaps those missionaries assigned to Japan had the most unusual experience. During this time, the Assemblies of God had one missionary caught in the cross fires of war, a single woman named Jessie Wengler. Wengler was born in Missouri in 1887. She first left for Japan in 1919.

Wengler's autobiography titled, *Letters from Japan*, paints an interesting picture for those who had labored there before the war. In a letter to a friend dated from 1933, Jessie relates the growing fear of war in Japan almost a decade before Pearl Harbor. "Cora Lee, these war clouds seem ominous to us over here. The undeclared war between Japan and China has stirred up a military fervor that is amazing."[206] In another letter Jessie describes the coming war like watching the clouds of a great storm gather on the horizon.

The rising tide of war caused most missionaries to leave Japan by the summer of 1941. Jessie, sick from overwork, anemia, and heart trouble was unable to be evacuated before Pearl Harbor was bombed.[207] She spent many months in a local hospital outside of Tokyo, before moving to a cooler climate in the mountains. When war was declared, her illness was greatly improved; but she still dealt with its effects each day.

Jessie was in route to a friend's home for a missionary get-together when the announcement came that war had been declared on America and Britain. Upon arriving, her friend shouted, "Oh, they are fighting, they are fighting."[208] All of those present at the meeting were now enemy nationals.

Following the start of the war, all American and British men were interned; however, women were placed under house arrest. Jessie once asked a Japanese officer checking in on her why she had not been interned. He replied, "America has not interned every Japanese and in return for that, we are leaving out a few Americans."[209] Military service in the early days of the war became mandatory. "There is no military exemption in Japan. Conscientious objectors are not known! We have been startled to hear that some of the pastors of our denomination have been called into military service."[210]

During this time, there were no means of communication with the United States. Jessie received one telegram from the Assemblies of God missions department and one letter from a relative. Her home was thoroughly searched by Japanese authorities. The only radio she owned was torn apart. "Less than a week after war was declared, five plain-clothes detectives came to my home and bowed themselves into the entrance. They came quietly and courteously and told me that they were sorry, they did not want to do what they had to do, but they had had orders to search all American houses."[211]

Food shortages began immediately. Already sick, Jessie was unable to obtain enough nutritious food to aid her condition. Her weight dropped to between 85 and 90 pounds. When food became scarce, those in Japan would drink tea. This helped curb their hunger during the worst times. By the end of the war, near famine conditions were found throughout Japan. Still, many natives brought food to her out of thanks for her friendship and all that she had done for them. Eggs, potatoes, grapes, and cheese helped to keep her alive. Surprisingly, the military allotted her the same amount of food as the Japanese people.

At first, Jessie was allowed to live at her own home, leaving only to obtain food. Later, they placed her with five other American missionaries. This lasted for a year. During this time, fuel became very scarce. Keeping warm was very difficult and cooking became a real problem. Charcoal was rationed; but often, the rationed amount was not available. Labor conscription also came to all like hunger and the lack of heat.

As the American bombers made runs over Japan, Jessie and her missionary colleagues found themselves in great danger. They longed for the war to be over but were torn as they watched thousands of Japanese die.

> The bombings of Tokyo became a very serious part of our days and nights. From November, 1944, to the end of the war, the American B-29's, B-24's and P-51's came over Tokyo almost every day and night. Three and four hundred at a time, and each time they came they dropped incendiary bombs and in some places demolition bombs. Pamphlets were dropped from the sky before these raids telling the Japanese that they were coming. District after district Tokyo was leveled by bombing and fire that followed.
>
> By the end of these raids, three fourths of the city was destroyed. The population of Tokyo at that time was seven million people. One hundred and sixteen other Japanese cities had the same fate.[212]

The war came to a speedy halt after the atomic bombs fell. On August 7, 1945, the emperor spoke to the nation for the first time via radio. His message was short. Japan was defeated. It would be an unconditional surrender. The American occupying force quickly came to their aid. Food and the necessities of life were now more prevalent. Some Christian servicemen even gave money to help rebuild the bombed out churches. "Instead of kindness, the Japanese had expected furious, wrathful vengeance from their Conquerors, but now realized their fears were unfounded."[213]

Following the end of the war, Jessie made plans to visit friends in Kofu, Japan. On her way, she stopped at a checkpoint to ask permission to travel. The Japanese gentleman said, "You do not need to have permission now to go. You are the victor, we are defeated. From now on we must ask your permission to carry on."[214]

A few weeks following the end of the war, Jessie and seventeen other missionaries received an invitation to come to the royal residence of Prince Higashi Kuni, cousin to the emperor. His request was simple. He asked them to "continue their work in Japan and to lead the people in a path of righteousness and bring them to God."[215]

General MacArthur visited Japan shortly after the surrender. In his opinion, the Japanese problem was theological. He stated his method as, "to sow an idea, the idea of freedom, the freedom which roots in religion."[216] To that Jessie states, "Free speech, free thought, free press, free religion—the four freedoms were brought to Japan."[217]

Because of health conditions, Jessie returned to the United States. She was in good company for part of the trip. General George Marshall and his staff were onboard the same plane. When they arrived at the military base, he requested that the ladies on the plane use his limousine; he and his men would go by Jeep.

"It was a beautiful, bright Sunday morning, January 6, 1946, when the US troopship *General Collins* arrived in San Francisco...I was on board that ship and I don't think any man felt more like shouting than I did."[218] After a few years of rest, Jessie returned to Japan in 1947. She remained there until her death from cancer in 1958. Her love for the people of Japan was not marred by the trials she endured at their hands. She was willing to return to their culture even in retirement.

CONCLUSION

The aftermath of war is the story of rebuilding—the rebuilding of cities, villages, and homes; the rebuilding of families, lives, and health; the rebuilding of dreams for the future and the promise of peace. It is also a time to reflect on the value of life and the strength that has been forged through adversity. Families welcome home loved ones, both civilians and soldiers. Others bury their loved ones with the honor that is due their service.

Throughout the Pacific the Japanese left a trail of terror and death in its wake. Thousands of lives were lost and billions of dollars of damage done. The brutality of the Japanese soldier was evident in the torture of prisoners. Suicide was a common occurrence by Japanese soldiers as the emperor's enemies tightened the rope of defeat around their necks. Those caught in the fighting found themselves living unimaginable horrors. Prisoners of war are expected, soldiers from opposing armies are often captured on the field of battle.

For many civilians moving into a different culture, learning its ways, and loving its people motivate them to go—be it doctor, nurse, or missionary, called by something bigger than themselves. For the doctors and nurses, it is a call to help the wounded and aid the sick. For the missionary, it is a call to reach the masses with a message of faith, putting their very lives on the line for the calling that they believe in.

It is fortunate for us living across time that they have left stories of their trials. Approaching the topic from their point of view can be difficult as details are pieced together from letters, missionary files, first-person articles and books, material written by other historians, as well as accounts from the soldiers that fought. Their lives serve as a beacon of hope to those of us who have never lived through such hardship. It is a story of a generation that rose up and overcame. They are stories that inspire us and move us.

While the Assemblies of God missionaries were the focus in this book, hundreds of other missionaries from all denominations lived the same story of hardship. The intention was to focus on those within the Assemblies of God and compliment their accounts with stories from others that they lived among within the concentration camps and missionary compounds.

Lives such as Rufus Grey the Baptist missionary that lost his life while being tortured in Baguio, Philippines, or the sisters from the Catholic convent just outside that city must be remembered. There was the Presbyterian missionary who read to Rena Baldwin as she lay sick in bed. While there are many divisions which separate denomination from denomination in these times of war, they were united around one common experience and cause, survival.

In the Philippines, we gain a picture of the pure brutality of the Japanese. Their use of torture to procure information and the intentional lack of food in the camps allow the reader to see the worst of the war. The stories related to Los Baños and the systematic killing of thousands of Filipino civilians only add to our horror.

Pictures of the death march participants move across our minds as the missionaries relate the scene at Old Bilibid Prison where so many American boys forced to march were buried. Others hear the shouts of triumph as General MacArthur rolls into the camp to see for himself the destruction of those he was forced to leave behind.

We breathe a sigh of relief when we understand the gravity of the Los Baños rescue and that not one prisoner was lost in the rescue. Surely this rivals the scenes of the greatest war movies ever made. Yet we realize that we are dealing with reality, not myth. For others, questions may arise. What if the paratroopers that dropped into Los Baños were fifteen minutes later? Would any of the interned have survived?

In China, we see a picture of diverging philosophies. Yes, internment came for most missionaries; however, their treatment differed greatly from those in the Philippines. Release came to some in China in the form of prisoner exchanges. Repatriation was never considered in the Philippines. In China, hundreds reached safety through escape across the vastness of the nation. Food shortages occurred but not to the same level.

In the internment camps in China missionaries fared far better than those in the Philippines. Families were allowed to stay together rather than not even being able to speak to each other across the camp. Hospital supplies were in far greater supply. Even the local Chinese were allowed to sell food to those interned.

In China, it would seem the greatest Japanese animosity was reserved for the natives. Their mutual hatred escalated skirmishes into all-out war. The Japanese held nothing back in dealing with the native people of China. Mass murder, rape, and robbery were as prevalent here as in the Philippines. For whatever reason, they chose to deal less harshly with enemy nationals not of Chinese descent. Some were even allowed to remain in their homes.

Perhaps the most baffling of all is the treatment of the missionary that remained in Japan. Having read accounts from other areas, execution for her would not be outside the realm of possibility. Yet, they chose to leave her alone. She suffered as the Japanese people suffered. As they ran short of food, she did also. When the bombs rained down from the sky, her life was in as much danger as her neighbors.

Whatever the challenges, each missionary had their own experiences at the hands of the Japanese. None counted it as a pleasurable time for them; but many viewed it as the perfect will of God for their lives. Their willingness to treat their captors with respect testifies of that belief. While most of the missionaries returned home to the United States following their release, for many it was only temporary. Their hope and their desire was to return to the peoples and cultures they loved so dearly.

In many cases, they were able to help the nations heal from its wounds of war. With the help of missionary societies and donors around the world, these heroes of faith were instrumental in the feeding of the hungry, the clothing of the naked, and the rebuilding of Christian communities throughout Asia. It was their calling.

Their lives and their stories are forever entwined. It is for future generations to learn the lessons that their experiences teach us. In a time of great up evil and turmoil, these missionaries lived life as best they could in the worst of circumstances. Being captured by the rising sun forever changed their lives.

BIBLIOGRAPHY

"1940s World War II Last-minute deliverance from execution." *The Pentecostal Evangel.* Springfield, July 20, 2003.

"1944 Press Release Lula Bell Hough." Assemblies of God Missionary File, Setpember 9, 1944.

"1958 Press Release for Miss Alice Stewart." Assemblies of God Missionary File, 1958.

"1962 Press Release Miss Alice Stewart." Assemblies of God Missionary File, December 1962.

"A Peaceful Spot in China." Assemblies of God Missionary File, September 20, 1941.

"A Teenager Growing Up at the Los Banos Camp." *Heritage.* Springfield, Spring 2005.

"After Pearl Harbor." Assemblies of God Missionary File.

Alcantara, Rosando. "Surviving the War in the Philippines." *Heritage*, Winter 1991-92: 6.

Alcantara, Rosendo. "Letter to Wayne Warner." Kahului, HI, February 1, 1985.

Appleby, Blanche. "God answers prayer to heal and deliver." *The Pentecostal Evangel.* Springfield, December 14, 1997.

Appleby, Blanche. "Our Remarkable Deliverance from Los Banos Internment Camp." *The Pentecostal Evangel.* Springfield, June 16, 1945.

Arthur, Anthony. *Deliverance At Los Banos.* New York: St. Martin's Press, 1985.

Astor, Gerald. *The Greatest War: Americans in Combat 1941-1945.* Novato: Presidio Press Inc., 1999.

Baldwin, Blanche Appleby and Rena. "Our Remarkable Deliverance from Los Banos Internment Camp." *The Pentecostal Evangel*, June 16, 1945: 1, 4-5.

Baldwin, Rena. "Hand Drawn Map of Central Luzon." Assemblies of God Missionary File, Around 1945.

Baldwin, Rena. "Letter." Assemblies of God Missionary File, Before 1945.

Baldwin, Rena. "Philippines." Assemblies of God Missionary File, After 1945.

Baldwin, Rena. "Somwehere in the Philippines." *The Herald: Camp Worship Program.* Assemblies of God Missionary File, March 4, 1945.

Baltau, Fred E. "Tientsin, China." Assemblies of God Missioanry File, February 23, 1946.

Barnaby, Catherine. "The Night Before Christmas: Los Banos Camp, '44." Assemblies of God Missioanry File, 1944.

"Biographical Sketch: Howard C. and Edith B. Osgood." Assemblies of God Missionary File, After 1959.

Blake, Gilson G. "Letter: From State Department concrning Leland Johnson." Assemblies of God Missionary File, April 4, 1945.

Blan, Nora. "Missionary Called Home." *The Pentecostal Evangel,* May 14, 1961.

Bradley, James. *Flags of Our Fathers.* New York: Bantam Books, 2000.

Brock, R. T. "Abigail Slager Called Home." Assemblies of God Missioanry File, November 1, 1959.

Brock, R.T. "Veteran China Missionary With the Lord." *The Pentecostal Evangel*, February 24, 1963: 26.

Brooks, Cyril H. "Rescue By Paratroopers." Assemblies of God Missionary File, February 1945.

Carlow, Margaret. "The King's Daughter: Jessie Wengler." *Heroes of the Conquest Series # 19*. Springfield, 1966.

Carlow, Margret. "Passing Through the Storm: Jessie Wengler." Assemblies of God Missionary File.

Carmichael, Christine. "Outpost of Democracy." *Pentecostal Evangel*, February 28, 1960: 19-20.

Dalton, Adele Flower. "From These Beginnings: Jessie Wengler." Assemblies of God Missionary File.

Dalton, Adele Flower. "Mother Peace." *Heritage*, Winter 1997-98: 22-25, 30.

Drez, Ronald J. *Twenty-Five Yards of War*. New York: Hyperion, 2001.

Dunnigan, James F. *The World War II Bookshelf*. New York: Citadel Press, 2004.

Eisenhower, John S. D. *Allies: Pearl Harbor to D-Day*. New York: Da Capo Press, 2000.

Ezzo, Elsie Bolton. "Beyond the Mekong." *Heroes of the Conquest Series #6*. Foreign Missions Dept. of the Assemblies of God, August 1961.

Fenby, Jonathan. *Alliance*. San Francisco: MacAdam Cage, 2006.

Finlay, Thelma. "Just Married: Mr. and Mrs. Slager." Assemblies of God Missioanry File, April 1961.

"Fred Baltau and Family in Japanese Internment Reported Well." Assemblies of God Missionary File, December 25, 1943.

Friedman, Ina R. *The Other Victims: First-Person Stories of Non-Jews Persecuted by the Navis.* Boston: Houghton Mifflin Company, 1990.

"From Japanese-Occupied Territory." *The Pentecostal Evangel.* July 17, 1943.

"From Tienstin, North China." Assemblies of God Missionary File, February 13, 1943.

Galley, Elizabeth. "Interned Missionary Writes Home." Assemblies of God Missioanry File, March 18, 1944.

Gee, Donald. "In Europe with Donald Gee, 1939." *Heritage*, Summer 1987: 13-14.

Glusman, John A. *Conduct Under Fire.* New York: Viking, 2005.

Gohr, Glenn. "Pioneer Missionaries to China Still Active in Springfield." *Heritage*, Fall 1988: 17, 20.

Greenaway, Charles E. "A Little Woman. A Big God." *The Evangelist.* August 1986.

Hansen, B. "Letter to Mother." Assemblies of God Missionary File, March 24, 1943.

Hansen, B. "Letter to Parents." Assemblies of God Missionary File, March 21, 1943.

Hansen, H. E. "Aboard the Motorship Gripsholm." Assemblies of God Missionary File, December 25, 1943.

Hansen, H.E. "Letter to Noel Perkin." Assemblies of God Missioanry File, May 15, 1942.

Hansen, Harold E. "Repatriated on the M.S. "Gripsholm"." Assemblies of God Missionary File, January 1, 1944.

Harris, Thomas S. "Letter: Concerning Rena Baldwin Medical Exam." Assemblies of God Missionary File, June 27, 1946.

Hindle, Thomas. "The Hindle Family." *Missionary Adventures.* Assemblies of God Missionary File, April 4, 1944.

Hogan, J. Philip. "The Dust of Shansi." *The Pentecostal Evangel.* Springfield, July 24, 1994.

"Honoring Lula Baird." *Printed from U.S. Missions Web Site.* Assemblies of God Missioanry File, December 11, 2008.

Hough, Lula Bell. "A Brief of Missionary Work in South China." Assemblies of God Missionary File, September 1951.

Hough, Lula Bell. "God Taught Her to Read." Assemblies of God Missionary File, April 1946.

Hough, Lula Bell. "Now It Can Be Told." Assemblies of God Missionary File, November 3, 1945.

Hough, Lula Bell. "Return to Fan Ling." Assemblies of God Missionary File, December 21, 1946.

Immell, Myra H. *World War II.* San Diego: Greenhaven Press, Inc., 2001.

"In Memory: Alice F. Stewart." Assemblies of God Missionary File, 1994.

Jakobson, Linda. *A Million Truths: A Decade in China.* New York: M. Evans and Company, Inc., 1998.

"Japanese Registration: Rena Baldwin." Assemblies of God Missionary File, August 9, 1943.

Johnson, Forrest Bryant. *Hour of Redemption: The Heroic WWII Saga of America's Most Daring POW Rescue.* New York: Warner Books, Inc., 2002.

Johnson, Leland E. *I Was Prisoner of the Japs.* Glendale: The Church Press, 1946.

Jones, Wilma. "Veteran Missionary Called Home: Henrietta Tieleman." Assemblies of God Missionary File, April 15, 1962.

Juergensen, Marie. "Ministering to Japanese-Americans in the Northwest." *Heritage*, Spring 1985: 7.

Kennedy, David M. *The Library of Congress World War II Companion.* New York: Simon and Schuster, 2007.

Kennedy, John W. "P.O.W. Former prisoner of war still a missionary at 85." *The Pentecostal Evangel.* Springfield, November 10, 2002.

Kvamme, B. Martin, Interview by Raymong Brock. *Answer to Ten Questions*, May 1, 1961.

Kvamme, B. "Under Japanese Rule." Assemblies of God Missionary File, October 1947.

Lindsay, Rena Baldwin. "Peace in the Day of Trouble." *The Pentecostal Evangel*, July 9, 1967: 26-27.

Maempa, John T. "Beginnings in Hong Kong." *Mountain Movers*, March 1997: 10-11.

Mathis, Frank F. *G.I. Jive: An Army Bandsman in World War II.* Lexington: The University Press of Kentucky, 1982.

McGee, Gary B. "Pentecostal Missionaries in Situations of Conflict and Violence." *Heritage.* Springfield, Summer 1992.

McManus, John C. *The Deadly Brotherhood: The American Combat Soldier in World War II.* Novato: Presidio Press, 1998.

Merson, John. *The Genius That Was China.* Woodstock: The Overlook Press, 1990.

Miller, Russell. *Behind the Lines.* New York: St. Martin's Press, 2002.

"Miss Alice F. Stewart News Release." Assemblies of God Missionary Files, Around 1964.

"Mongolia Missionary With the Lord: Louise Hindle." Assemblies of God Missionary File, June 28, 1964.

Morris, Eric. *Corregidor: The American Alamo of World War II.* 1981: Cooper Square Press, New York.

Mullener, Elizabeth. *War Stories: Rembering World War II.* Baton Rouge: Louisiana State University Press, 2002.

Netherlands, Consulate of the. "Letter." Assemblies of God Missionary File, October 25, 1956.

"News Flash: Slager." Assemblies of God Missionary File, October 23, 1943.

"News Release: Baltaus." Assemblies of God Missionary File, September 22, 1945.

"News Release: Bolton." Assemblies of God Missionary File, January 12, 1946.

North, Oliver. *War Stories II: The Heroes Who Defeated Hitler.* Washington D.C.: Regnery Publishing, Inc., 2005.

O'Donnell, Patrick K. *Into the Rising Sun.* New York : The Free Press, 2002.

Office, Associated Mission Medical. "Medical Examination: George Slager." Assemblies of God Missionary File, September 4, 1947.

"Osgood Biography." Assemblies of God Missionary File, After 1992.

Osgood, Howard C. ""Jesus is Still Left to Us"." *The Pentecostal Evangel.* Springfield, September 26, 1942.

Osgood, Howard C. ""Under His Wings Shalt Thou Turst"." *The Pentecostal Evangel.* Springfield, August 29, 1942.

Osgood, Howard C. "Bombs and Blessings in Yunnan." *The Pentecostal Evangel.* Springfield, December 31, 1938.

Osgood, Howard C. "Fleeing the Bombs in Kunming, China." *Heritage.* Assemblies of God Missionary File, Winter 2001-2002.

Park, Harland. "Autobiography of H. A. Park." Assemblies of God Missionary File, After 1942.

PBS. *PBS.* 2009. http://www.pbs.org/wgbh/amex/macarthur/filmmore/reference/primary/macspeech02.html (accessed October 7, 2010).

Pearson, Judith L. *Belly of the Beast.* New York: New American Library, 2001.

Pegues, Kathy. "Missionary Back Home to Retire." Assemblies of God Missionary File, Around 1975.

Perdue, John. "In Perils of the Sea." *The Pentecostal Evangel.* 9 November, 1946.

Perdue, John. "In Perils Often." *The Pentecostal Evangel.* November 2, 1946.

Perdue, John. "My most un-forgettable experience." 1941.

Perdue, John. "Praying Behind Barbed Wire." Assemblies of God Missioanry File, July 1960.

Perdue, John. "Under His Wings." *The Pentecostal Evangel.* December 21, 1946.

"Philippine Flash." Assemblies of God Missionary File, August 5, 1944.

Philippine History. January 18, 2010. http://www.philippine-history.org/japanese-occupation.htm (accessed 4 2010, October).

Plymire, V. G. "Letter to Noel Perkin." Assemblies of God Missionary File, April 15, 1943.

Raile, Colonel R. E. "Letter: Award Declaration." Assemblies of God Missionary File, May 1, 1945.

Ray, John. *The Second World War.* London: Cassell, 1999.

Rees, Laurence. *Horror in the East: Japan and the Atrocities of World War II.* Cambridge: Da Capo Press, 2001.

"Refugee Work." Assemblies of God Missionary File, Park, December 1, 1940.

Rennell, John Nichol and Tony. *The Last Escape: The Untold Story of Allied Prisoners of War In Europe 1944-45.* New York: Viking, 2002.

"Repatriation Ship Newspaper." *Eberle Echo: A Daily of the Ship, by the Ship, for the Ship.* Assemblies of God Missioanry File, April 23, 1945.

Rooney, Andy. *My War.* New York: Random House, 1995.

"Safe." Assemblies of God Missioanry File, Slager, November 24, 1945.

"Safe in China." Assemblies of God Missionary File, January 31, 1942.

Schmidt, G. Herbert. *Songs in the Night.* Springfield: Gospel Publishing House, 1945.

Scull, Paul E. "Miracles in World War II P.O.W. Camps." *Heritage*, 2009: 53-55.

Sides, Hampton. *Ghost Soldiers: The Forgotten Epic Story of World War II's Most Dramatic Mission.* New York : Doubleday, 2001.

Slager, George C. "Letter to B. G. Foote." Assemblies of God Missioanry File, November 8, 1956.

Sloan, Bill. *The Ultimate Battle.* New York: Simon and Schuster, 2007.

Smith, Goerky. "Looking Back: God is Faithful." *Live*, December 15, 1996.

Smith, Judy Barrett and Litoff, David C. *Since You Went Away: World War II Letters From American Women on the Home Front.* New York: Oxford University Press, 1991.

Smith, Steven Trent. *The Rescue.* New York: John Wiley & Sons, Inc., 2001.

Sorel, Nancy Caldwell. *The Women Who Wrote the War.* New York: Arcade Publishing, 1999.

Spector, Ronald E. *Eagale Against the Sun: The American War with Japan.* New York: Vintage Books, 1985.

Spence, Inez. "Woman of Courage: Marie Stephany." *Heroes of the Conquest Series #12*, After 1962.

State, Department of. "Letter to General Council of Assemblies of God: Gladys Knowles." Assemblies of God Missionary File, December 13, 1943.

Stephany, Marie. *The Dragon Defeated.* Word and Witness Publishing Co.

Stewart, Alice. "Jesus Loves Me." July 3, 1946.

Stewart, Alice. "Peter's God Still Lives." Assemblies of God Missionary Files, February 23, 1946.

Stewart, Alice. "The Sheep of His Pasture." Assemblies of God Missionary File, November 26, 1961.

"Still On the Firing Line." Assemblies of God Missionary File, March 21, 1942.

Tangen, Mildred, interview by Adele Dalton. *Mildred Tangen/ Taiwan*, February 7, 1980.

Tangen, Robert B. "Did You Pray." *The Pentecostal Evangel.* Springfield, January 12, 1946.

Tangen, Robert. "Letter to Noel Perkin." Assemblies of God Missionary File, April 14, 1945.

Taylor, William. *Rescued By Mao.* Sandy: Silverleaf Press, 2007.

"Teacher Saved From Japs To PSeak Here Tomorrow." *Springfield, MO Newspaper.* Springfield, Summer 1945.

The Pentecostal Evangel. "Our Interest in the Philippines." January 3, 1942: 8-9.

"Thelma Virginia Hildebrand Biography." Assemblies of God Missioanry File, Around 1988.

Tieleman, Henrietta. "Beyond the West Gate Mission: Those Fingers." Assemblies of God Missionary File, After 1947.

Tieleman, Henrietta, interview by Assemblies of God Foreign Missions. *Interview*, After 1952.

Tieleman, Henrietta. "Our Last Day in Ta Chang." Assemblies of God Missionary Files, March 25, 1944.

"U.S. Dept. of Labor: Medical Report for Rena Baldwin." Assemblies of God Missionary File, December 8, 1941.

"War Mercies." Assemblies of God Missioanry File, Slager, January 12, 1946.

Warner, Wayne. "A Christmas surprise in a World War II prison camp." *The Pentecostal Evangel.* Springfield, December 24, 2000.

Warner, Wayne E. "1945 Philippine Liberation Creates Emotional Scene." *Heritage*, Spring 1985: 6-12.

Warner, Wayne. "GIs rescue missionaries in the Philippines during World War II." *The Pentecostal Evangel.* Springfield, March 26, 1995.

Warner, Wayne. "50 Years Ago." *Heritage*, Winter 1991-92: 2-3.

Warner, Wayne. "A Refugee in Sweden." *Heritage*, Spring 1992: 3-5, 24.

Warner, Wayne. "An American Missionary in Nazi Hands: The Story of G. Herbert Schmidt in Danzig." *Heritage*, Winter 1991-92: 10-11, 27.

Warner, Wayne. "Missionaries Caught in the Crossfire." *Heritage*, Winter 1991-92: 4-9, 26-27.

Warner, Wayne. "The Dramatic 1945 Liberation at Los Banos, Philippines." *Heritage*, Summer 1985: 7-11.

Warner, Wayne. "Missionaries Celebrate the True Spirit of Christmas." *Pentecostal Evangel*, December 31, 1995: 27.

Warner, Wayne. "The Dramatic World War II Liberation at Los Banos." *Heritage.* Springfield, Spring 2005.

Wengler, Jessie. "Delivered from Destruction in Tokyo." *Heritage*, Spring 1985: 6.

Wengler, Jessie. *Letters from Japan.* Pasadena: Self, 1946.

Wengler, Jessie. "Delivered from Destruction in Tokyo." *The Pentecostal Evangel*, February 23, 1946: 1, 10-14.

Wilson, Elizabeth A. *Life in a Japanese Internement Camp.* Thesis, Fort Worth: Texas Christian University, 1967.

Wilson, Elizabeth Galley. "A Special Christmas Eve in Peking." *Heritage*, Winter 1982-83: 2.

Wilson. Elizabeth Galley. "War Reaches Baguio, Philippine Islands." *Heritage.* Springfield, Winter 2001-2002.

Wilson, Elizabeth. *Making Many Rich.* Springfield: Gospel Publishing House, 1955.

"With Christ: George C. Slager." Assemblies of God Missioanry File, January 19, 1969.

"With Christ: Thomas Hindle." Assemblies of God Missionary File, September 28, 1969.

Wolter, Tim. *POW Baseball in World War II.* Jefferson: McFarlans and Company, Inc., Publishers, 2002.

Young, Donald J. *The Battle of Bataan.* Jefferson: McFarland & Company, Inc., Publishers, 1992.

ENDNOTES

THE PHILIPPINES

1   Elizabeth A Wilson, *Life in a Japanese Internement Camp Thesis* (Fort Worth: Texas Christian University, 1967).

2   Corregidor is an island at the entrance to Manila Bay.

3   James Bradley, *Flags of Our Fathers* (New York: Bantam Books, 2000).

4   John S. D. Eisenhower, *Allies: Pearl Harbor to D-Day* (New York: Da Capo Press, 2000), 8.

5   Eisenhower, *Allies*, 13.

6   President Taft served as the head of the Philippine commission from 1900-1901.

7   Anthony Arthur, *Deliverance At Los Baños* (New York: St. Martin's Press, 1985), 12.

8   Arthur, *Deliverance*, 12.

9   General Eisenhower became the Supreme Commander of the Allied forces in Europe and the future President of the United States, elected in 1952.

10 Elizabeth Mullener, *War Stories: Rembering World War II* (Baton Rouge: Louisiana State University Press, 2002), 77.

11 Ronald E. Spector, *Eagale Against the Sun: The American War with Japan* (New York: Vintage Books, 1985), 69.

12 Elizabeth A Wilson, *Life in a Japanese Internement Camp Thesis* (Fort Worth: Texas Christian University, 1967), 2.

13 John S. D Eisenhower, *Allies: Pearl Harbor to D-Day* (New York: Da Capo Press, 2000), 18.

14 Ronald E. Spector, *Eagle Against the Sun: The American War with Japan* (New York: Vintage Books, 1985), 74.

15 John Ray, *The Second World War* (London: Cassell, 1999), 144.

16 John C McManus, *The Deadly Brotherhood: The American Combat Soldier in World War II* (Novato: Presidio Press, 1998), 81.

17 PBS. *PBS*. 2009. http://www.pbs.org/wgbh/amex/macarthur/filmmore/reference/primary/macspeech02.html (accessed October 7, 2010).

18   John S. D. Eisenhower, *Allies: Pearl Harbor to D-Day* (New York: Da Capo Press, 2000), 50.

19   Jonathan Fenby, *Alliance* (San Francisco: MacAdam Cage, 2006), 96.

20   Anthony Arthur, *Deliverance At Los Baños* (New York: St. Martin's Press, 1985), 15.

21   Elizabeth Mullener, *War Stories: Rembering World War II* (Baton Rouge: Louisiana State University Press, 2002), 68.

22   Nancy Caldwell Sorel, *The Women Who Wrote the War* (New York: Arcade Publishing, 1999), 153.

23   Elizabeth Mullener, *War Stories: Rembering World War II* (Baton Rouge: Louisiana State University Press, 2002), 70.

24   David M Kennedy, *The Library of Congress World War II Companion* (New York: Simon and Schuster, 2007), 173.

25   Kennedy, *Liberty of Congress World War II Companion*, 181.

26   Anthony Arthur, *Deliverance At Los Baños* (New York: St. Martin's Press, 1985).

27   Arthur, *Deliverance At Los Baños*, xi.

28   AG Missionary File Cover

29   Rosendo Alcantara, "Letter to Wayne Warner." (Kahului, HI, February 1, 1985), 1.

30   Sister Baldwin and Sister Appleby are the names Leland Johnson used in his book. They are Rena Baldwin and Blanche Appleby

31   Leland E Johnson, *I Was Prisoner of the Japs* (Glendale: The Church Press, 1946), 18.

32   Johnson, *I Was Prisoner of the Japs*, 23.

33   Johnson, *I Was Prisoner of the Japs*, 25.

34   Johnson, *I Was Prisoner of the Japs*.

35   Johnson, *I Was Prisoner of the Japs*.

36   Johnson, *I Was Prisoner of the Japs*, 47.

37   Johnson, *I Was Prisoner of the Japs*.

38   The water-cure was a form of torture where a three foot hose was placed into the victim's stomach via his mouth. Water was then poured into the stomach until it protruded. Once this was accomplished the soldier would then jump on the victim's stomach until he would talk or was dead.

39   Tim Wolter, *POW Baseball in World War II* (Jefferson: McFarlans and Company, Inc., Publishers, 2002).

40   Leland E Johnson, *I Was Prisoner of the Japs* (Glendale: The Church Press, 1946, 120).

41 Judith L Pearson, *Belly of the Beast* (New York: New American Library, 2001), 85.

42 Pearson, *Belly of the Beast*, 84.

43 Pearson, *Belly of the Beast*, 87.

44 Leland E Johnson, *I Was Prisoner of the Japs* (Glendale: The Church Press, 1946), 128.

45 Johnson, *I Was Prisoner of the Japs*.

46 Gerald Astor, *The Greatest War: Americans in Combat 1941-1945* (Novato: Presidio Press Inc., 1999), 175.

47 Leland E Johnson, *I Was Prisoner of the Japs* (Glendale: The Church Press, 1946), 133.

48 Johnson, *I Was Prisoner of the Japs*, 135.

49 Johnson, *I Was Prisoner of the Japs*, 137.

50 Gerald Astor, *The Greatest War: Americans in Combat 1941-1945* (Novato: Presidio Press Inc., 1999), 825.

51 Astor, *The Greatest War*.

52 Leland E Johnson, *I Was Prisoner of the Japs* (Glendale: The Church Press, 1946), 143.

53 Wayne Warner, "The Dramatic World War II Liberation at Los Banos." *Heritage* (Springfield, Spring 2005), 39.

54 Elizabeth Galley Wilson, "War Reaches Baguio, Philippine Islands." *Heritage* (Springfield, Winter 2001-2002), 12.

55 Wilson, "War Reaches Baguio, Philippine Islands." *Heritage*.

56 Elizabeth A Wilson, *Life in a Japanese Internement Camp. Thesis* (Fort Worth: Texas Christian University, 1967), 1.

57 Wilson, *Life in a Japanese Internement Camp. Thesis*, 2.

58 Eric Morris,.*Corregidor: The American Alamo of World War II* (New York: Cooper Square Press, 1981), 163.

59 Elizabeth A Wilson, *Life in a Japanese Internement Camp. Thesis* (Fort Worth: Texas Christian University, 1967), 5.

60 Wilson, *Life in a Japanese Internement Camp. Thesis*, 6.

61 Wilson, *Life in a Japanese Internement Camp. Thesis*, 7.

62 Wilson, *Life in a Japanese Internement Camp. Thesis*, 8.

63 Mildred Tangen, interview by Adele Dalton, *Mildred Tangen/Taiwan* (February 7, 1980), 7.

64 Elizabeth A Wilson, *Life in a Japanese Internement Camp. Thesis* (Fort Worth: Texas Christian University, 1967), 14.

65 Wilson, *Life in a Japanese Internement Camp. Thesis*, 16.

66 Elizabeth A Wilson, *Life in a Japanese Internement Camp. Thesis* (Fort Worth: Texas Christian University, 1967), 17.

67   Elizabeth Galley, "Interned Missionary Writes Home." Assemblies of God Missioanry File, (March 18, 1944).

68   Elizabeth A Wilson, *Life in a Japanese Internement Camp. Thesis* (Fort Worth: Texas Christian University, 1967), 21.

69   Wayne Warner, "Missionaries Celebrate the True Spirit of Christmas." *Pentecostal Evangel*, (December 31, 1995), 27.

70   Eric Morris, *Corregidor: The American Alamo of World War II* (New York: Cooper Square Press, 1981), 412.

71   Morris, *Corregidor*, 490.

72   Morris, *Corregidor*, 479.

73   Elizabeth A Wilson, *Life in a Japanese Internement Camp. Thesis* (Fort Worth: Texas Christian University, 1967), 37.

74   Wilson, *Life in a Japanese Internement Camp. Thesis*, 38

75   Eric Morris, *Corregidor: The American Alamo of World War II* (New York: Cooper Square Press, 1981), 496.

76   Morris, *Corregidor*.

77   Mabuhay is an informal Tagolog word meaning welcome, used with friends.

78   Elizabeth A Wilson, *Life in a Japanese Internement Camp. Thesis* (Fort Worth: Texas Christian University, 1967), 38.

79   Wilson, *Life in a Japanese Internement Camp. Thesis*, 40.

80   Eric Morris, *Corregidor: The American Alamo of World War II* (New York: Cooper Square Press, 1981), 167-168.

81   Blanche Appleby, "Our Remarkable Deliverance from Los Banos Internment Camp." (The Pentecostal Evangel, Springfield, June 16, 1945), 4.

82   Appleby, "Our Remarkable Deliverance from Los Banos Internment Camp.", 4.

83   Appleby, "Our Remarkable Deliverance from Los Banos Internment Camp.", 5.

84   Anthony Arthur, *Deliverance At Los Baños* (New York: St. Martin's Press, 1985), 36.

85   Tim Wolter, *POW Baseball in World War II* (Jefferson: McFarlans and Company, Inc., Publishers, 2002).

86   Eric Morris, *Corregidor: The American Alamo of World War II* (New York: Cooper Square Press, 1981), 484.

87   Anthony Arthur, *Deliverance At Los Baños* (New York: St. Martin's Press, 1985), 37.

88   Tim Wolter, *POW Baseball in World War II* (Jefferson: McFarlans and Company, Inc., Publishers, 2002).

89   Ibid, 152.

90   Anthony Arthur, *Deliverance At Los Baños* (New York: St. Martin's Press, 1985), 50.

91   Blanche Appleby, "Our Remarkable Deliverance from Los Banos Internment Camp." (The Pentecostal Evangel, Springfield, June 16, 1945), 5.

92   Anthony Arthur, *Deliverance At Los Baños* (New York: St. Martin's Press, 1985).

93   Blanche Appleby, "Our Remarkable Deliverance from Los Banos Internment Camp." (The Pentecostal Evangel, Springfield, June 16, 1945), 5.

94   Anthony Arthur, *Deliverance At Los Baños* (New York: St. Martin's Press, 1985), 79.

95   Arthur, *Deliverance At Los Baños*, 97.

96   Arthur, *Deliverance At Los Baños*, 120-1.

97   Arthur, *Deliverance At Los Baños*, 126.

98   Arthur, *Deliverance At Los Baños*, 159.

99   Arthur, *Deliverance At Los Baños*, 129.

100 Arthur, *Deliverance At Los Baños*, 135.

101 Arthur, *Deliverance At Los Baños*, 191, 201.

102 Eric Morris, *Corregidor: The American Alamo of World War II* (New York: Cooper Square Press), 1981, 501.

103 Anthony Arthur, *Deliverance At Los Baños* (New York: St. Martin's Press, 1985), 202.

104 Gerald Astor, *The Greatest War: Americans in Combat 1941-1945* (Novato: Presidio Press Inc., 1999), 830.

105   Eric Morris, *Corregidor: The American Alamo of World War II* (New York: Cooper Square Press, 1981), 501.

106   Many Nuns from the Sisters of Maryknoll convent in Baguio were interned at Los Baños.

107   Eric Morris, *Corregidor: The American Alamo of World War II* (New York: Cooper Square Press, 1981), 502.

108   Gerald Astor, *The Greatest War: Americans in Combat 1941-1945* (Novato: Presidio Press Inc., 1999).

109   Blanche Appleby, "Our Remarkable Deliverance from Los Banos Internment Camp" (The Pentecostal Evangel, Springfield, June 16, 1945), 5.

110   Gerald Astor, *The Greatest War: Americans in Combat 1941-1945* (Novato: Presidio Press Inc., 1999), 831.

111   Amtrack stands for amphibian tractor.

112   Blanche Appleby, "Our Remarkable Deliverance from Los Banos Internment Camp" (The Pentecostal Evangel, Springfield, June 16, 1945), 5.

113   Anthony Arthur, *Deliverance At Los Baños* (New York: St. Martin's Press, 1985), 251.

114   Eric Morris, *Corregidor: The American Alamo of World War II.* (New York: Cooper Square Press, 1981), 503.

115   Blanche Appleby, "Our Remarkable Deliverance from Los Banos Internment Camp." (The Pentecostal Evangel, Springfield, June 16, 1945).

116   This is the only author that uses this spelling.

117   Eric Morris, *Corregidor: The American Alamo of World War II* (New York: Cooper Square Press, 1981), 500.

118   Beri-beri is an ailment of the nervous system often resulting in an enlarged heart.

119   Tropical sprue is a malabsorption disease resulting in severe diarrhea and intestinal problems.

120   Anthony Arthur,.*Deliverance At Los Baños* (New York: St. Martin's Press, 1985), 258.

121   Frank F Mathis, *G.I. Jive: An Army Bandsman in World War II* (Lexington: The University Press of Kentucky, 1982), 148.

122   Mathis, *G.I. Jive.*

123   Mathis, *G.I. Jive*, 132.

124   Kamikaze is the Japanese tactic of flying airplanes into enemy ships; the pilot willing to give his life for the empire.

125   Nancy Caldwell Sorel, *The Women Who Wrote the War* (New York: Arcade Publishing, 1999), 297.

126   John Ray, *The Second World War* (London: Cassell, 1999), 302.

127   Bill Sloan, *The Ultimate Battle* (New York: Simon and Schuster, 2007), 332.

128 John Ray, *The Second World War* (London: Cassell, 1999), 283.

129 Anthony Arthur, *Deliverance At Los Baños* (New York: St. Martin's Press, 1985), 183.

130 Arthur, *Deliverance At Los Baños*, 177.

131 Arthur, *Deliverance At Los Baños*, 183.

132 Arthur, *Deliverance At Los Baños*, 132.

133 Frank F Mathis, *G.I. Jive: An Army Bandsman in World War II* (Lexington: The University Press of Kentucky, 1982), 149.

134 Frank F Mathis, G.I. Jive: An Army Bandsman in World War II (Lexington: The University Press of Kentucky, 1982), 118.

135 Gerald Astor, *The Greatest War: Americans in Combat 1941-1945* (Novato: Presidio Press Inc., 1999), 820.

136 Astor, *The Greatest War*, 950.

137 Judy Barrett Smith and David C Litoff, *Since You Went Away: World War II Letters From American Women on the Home Front* (New York: Oxford University Press, 1991), 188.

138 John C McManus, *The Deadly Brotherhood: The American Combat Soldier in World War II* (Novato: Presidio Press, 1998), 92.

139 Judy Barrett Smith and David C Litoff, *Since You Went Away: World War II Letters From American Women on*

CAPTURED BY THE RISING SUN

the Home Front (New York: Oxford University Press, 1991), 229-230.

140   Smith and Litoff, *Since You Went Away*, 264.

141   John C McManus, *The Deadly Brotherhood: The American Combat Soldier in World War II* (Novato: Presidio Press, 1998), 177.

142   McManus, *The Deadly Brotherhood*, 165.

143   McManus, *The Deadly Brotherhood*, 132.

CHINA

144   John Merson, *The Genius That Was China* (Woodstock: The Overlook Press, 1990), 216.

145   Linda Jakobson, *A Million Truths: A Decade in China* (New York: M. Evans and Company, Inc., 1998), 272.

146   Laurence Rees, *Horror in the East: Japan and the Atrocities of World War II* (Cambridge: Da Capo Press, 2001), 27.

147   John A Glusman, *Conduct Under Fire* (New York: Viking, 2005), 283.

148   The Channel Islands are not a part of the United Kingdom, but are considered Crown dependencies.

149   Laurence Rees, *Horror in the East: Japan and the Atrocities of World War II* (Cambridge: Da Capo Press, 2001), 53.

150   Rees, *Horror in the East*, 65.

151   Rees, *Horror in the East*, 64.

152   Ronald J Drez, *Twenty-Five Yards of War* (New York: Hyperion, 2001).

153   Laurence Rees, *Horror in the East: Japan and the Atrocities of World War II* (Cambridge: Da Capo Press, 2001), 66.

154   Rees, *Horror in the East*, 69.

155   Rees, *Horror in the East*, 73.

156   Russell Miller, *Behind the Lines* (New York: St. Martin's Press, 2002), 244.

157   The Burma Road was an inland trade route connecting China to India through Burma.

158   Patrick K O'Donnell, *Into the Rising Sun* (New York : The Free Press, 2002), 150.

159   Ronald J Drez, *Twenty-Five Yards of War* (New York: Hyperion, 2001), 22.

160   John T Maempa, "Beginnings in Hong Kong." (Mountain Movers, March 1997: 10-11), 11.

161   Christine Carmichael, "Outpost of Democracy." (Pentecostal Evangel, February 28, 1960: 19-20), 19.

162   Harland Park, "Autobiography of H. A. Park." (Assemblies of God Missionary File, After 1942), 9.

163 John Perdue, "My most un-forgettable experience." (1941).

164 Harland Park, "Autobiography of H. A. Park." (Assemblies of God Missionary File, After 1942), 10.

165 John Perdue, "In Perils Often." (The Pentecostal Evangel. November 2, 1946).

166 Perdue, "In Perils Often.".

167 Goerky Smith, "Looking Back: God is Faithful." (Live, December 15, 1996), 2.

168 "1944 Press Release Lula Bell Hough." (Assemblies of God Missionary File, Setpember 9, 1944).

169 Paul E Scull, "Miracles in World War II P.O.W. Camps." (Heritage, 2009: 53-55), 55.

170 John Perdue, "In Perils Often." (The Pentecostal Evangel, November 2, 1946).

171 Harland Park, "Autobiography of H. A. Park." (Assemblies of God Missionary File, After 1942), 10.

172 Lula Bell Hough, "God Taught Her to Read." (Assemblies of God Missionary File, April 1946).

173 Harland Park, "Autobiography of H. A. Park." (Assemblies of God Missionary File, After 1942), 11.

174 John Perdue, "My most un-forgettable experience." (1941).

175   Harland Park, "Autobiography of H. A. Park." (Assemblies of God Missionary File, After 1942), 12.

176   "Refugee Work", (Assemblies of God Missionary File, Park, December 1, 1940).

177   John Perdue, "Praying Behind Barbed Wire." (Assemblies of God Missioanry File, July 1960).

178   The Swedish-American liner served as an International Red Cross exchange ship during World War II.

179   Kathy Pegues, "Missionary Back Home to Retire." (Assemblies of God Missionary File, Around 1975).

180   Goerky Smith, "Looking Back: God is Faithful." (Live, December 15, 1996), 6.

181   Free China was the area not yet controlled by the Communist Party.

182   Article info not given other than date of 9-9-1944.

183   John Perdue, "In Perils of the Sea." (The Pentecostal Evangel, November 9, 1946).

184   Nora Blan, "Missionary Called Home." (The Pentecostal Evangel, May 14, 1961).

185   R.T. Brock, "Veteran China Missionary With the Lord." (The Pentecostal Evangel, February 24, 1963), 26.

186   Alice Stewart, "Jesus Loves Me." (July 3, 1946).

187   Stewart, "Jesus Loves Me.".

188 Henrietta Tieleman, "Our Last Day in Ta Chang." (Assemblies of God Missionary Files, March 25, 1944).

189 "After Pearl Harbor." Assemblies of God Missionary File, Tieleman.

190 Thomas Hindle, "The Hindle Family." (Missionary Adventures. Assemblies of God Missionary File, April 4, 1944), 7.

191 Also spelled Wei Hsien

192 Thomas Hindle, "The Hindle Family." (Missionary Adventures. Assemblies of God Missionary File, April 4, 1944), 10.

193 Hindle, "The Hindle Family.", 11.

194 Hindle, "The Hindle Family.", 14.

195 Hindle, "The Hindle Family.", 15.

196 Hindle, "The Hindle Family.", 17.

197 Hindle, "The Hindle Family.", 25.

198 H. E. Hansen, "Aboard the Motorship Gripsholm." (Assemblies of God Missionary File, December 25, 1943).

199 "Safe." (Assemblies of God Missioanry File, Slager, November 24, 1945).

200 "Safe.".

201 Thelma Finlay, "Just Married: Mr. and Mrs. Slager." (Assemblies of God Missioanry File, April 1961).

202 "War Mercies." (Assemblies of God Missioanry File, Slager, January 12, 1946).

203 "Thelma Virginia Hildebrand Biography." (Assemblies of God Missioanry File, Around 1988).

204 Howard C Osgood, "Fleeing the Bombs in Kunming, China." (Heritage, Assemblies of God Missionary File, Winter 2001-2002).

205 John Perdue, "In Perils of the Sea." (The Pentecostal Evangel, November 9, 1946).

JAPAN

206 Jessie Wengler, *Letters from Japan,* (Pasadena: Self, 1946), 38.

207 Margaret Carlow, "The King's Daughter: Jessie Wengler." (Heroes of the Conquest Series #19. Springfield, 1966).

208 Jessie Wengler, *Letters from Japan,* (Pasadena: Self, 1946), 41.

209 Wengler, *Letters from Japan*, 47.

210 Wengler, *Letters from Japan*, 39.

211 Wengler, *Letters from Japan*, 42.

212 Wengler, *Letters from Japan*, 50.

213 Wengler, *Letters from Japan*, 51.

214 Wengler, *Letters from Japan*, 52.

215 Margaret Carlow, "The King's Daughter: Jessie Wengler." (Heroes of the Conquest Series # 19. Springfield, 1966), 13.

216 Jessie Wengler, *Letters from Japan,* (Pasadena: Self, 1946), 53.

217 Wengler, *Letters from Japan*, 53.

218 Wengler, *Letters from Japan*, 41.

Alice Stewart

Blanche Appleby and Rena Baldwin

H E Hansen Family

Fred Baltau

Mrs. Baltau

H A and Betty Parks

Mr. and Mrs. Howard Osgood

Rev. and Mrs. Leland E. Johnson
Constance and Samuel
Missionaries
at Dosing, South China

<table>
<tr><td>FOREIGN ADDRESS</td><td>HOME ADDRESS</td></tr>
<tr><td>P. O. Box 721</td><td>17 N. Wabash Ave.</td></tr>
<tr><td>Hong Kong</td><td>Battle Creek, Mich.</td></tr>
</table>

*Go ye therefore, and "make disciples of all nations,"
baptizing them in the name of the Father, and of the Son,
and of the Holy Spirit.*

*Teaching them to observe all things whatsoever I have
commanded you: and, lo, I am with you alway, even unto
the end of the world.—Matt. 28: 19,20.*

Pray for us

Leland Johnson Family Prayer Card

Leonard Bolton Family

Lula Bell Hough

Lula Bell Hough

Lula Baird

Mrs. Hindle

Thomas Hindle

Thelma Hildebrand